P9-EEH-545

A DOZEN
AND ONE

by

JIM TULLY

HOLLYWOOD
MURRAY & GEE, INC.
1943

MURRAY & GEE, INCORPORATED, *Publishers*
1622 NO. HIGHLAND, HOLLYWOOD, CALIF.

Copyright 1943
By JIM TULLY

Printed in the United States of America

To

ARNOLD GINGRICH

and

DAMON RUNYON

Without Whom . . .

ACKNOWLEDGEMENT

Acknowledgement is made to the following periodicals in which some of these sketches, in whole or in part, first appeared.

ESQUIRE

AMERICAN MERCURY
August 1933
LIBERTY

CONTENTS

Introducing . . .

JIM TULLY

By

DAMON RUNYON

INTRODUCTION

Jim Tully has slugged a typewriter from obscurity and poverty since hanging up the gloves. A former road kid and orphan, his fighting had the slap and dash of his writing. He has become a greater writer . . . one of the finest in America. We will put him among the first five anyway.

One of his books is dedicated to Jack Dempsey — his fellow road kid. It is one of the greatest distinctions Dempsey will ever attain. The two are close friends.

Jim Tully is unique. There is more life in five pages of him than in five hundred of many a highbrow who will be translated into ten languages. He has humanity, grand humor and a surge of emotional passions. His writing entertains me more than any fight I have ever watched. Its fineness induces me to tell all and sundry that they will lose something if they do not read him.

Jim might be termed a discovery of Rupert Hughes, that genial fellow who has always helped others! Hughes showed himself not only a splendid writer but critic when he said that Jim's descriptions of wild night rides had shown him that a new and powerful writer had entered the field of American literature. . . .

Jim is a short square built fellow with a head of hair like a fright wig. You wouldn't take him for a literary gent. A section foreman, yes. A bouncer in a Tenth Avenue ginnery, yes. A littérateur, no. He looks rough and tough, and able bodied. But he isn't tough, except physically. He is a nice fellow. There is a breath of the

INTRODUCTION

Ould Sod in his accent. But if occasion demands he can pull culture on you with the ease of an old fashioned town marshal getting out his six pistol. A great man in his own right, Jim is one of the finest living American authors. He is now about forty-five years old and looks younger. He was a bit of everything before he turned to writing—so he is pretty well equipped for writing about life.

I will step aside now for one of the greatest critics in America, H. L. Mencken, who says,

"If Jim Tully were a Russian, read in translation, all the professors would be hymning him. He has all of Gorky's capacity for making vivid the miseries of poor and helpless men, and in addition he has a humor that no Russian could conceivably have."

CHARLIE CHAPLIN

CHARLIE CHAPLIN

It has been nearly twenty years since I first met Charlie Chaplin at a dinner given by Ralph Block in Hollywood. A book upon which I had been working for over a decade had been accepted for publication. I was still dazed and poverty-stricken from the experience. Though the novel was sentimental and uneven, Block had faith that I might be more than a "one book man." As such, he brought me to Chaplin.

Paul Bern, a Prussian Jew, and the only man I have ever known who practiced the teachings of Christ, was a guest. Carey Wilson and others were also present.

Having learned to observe men during seven years as a road kid, and later as a wandering bruiser, I was soon aware that success had put a polish on the screen vagabond. If manners were a cloak to hide feelings, he wore a gorgeous garment. I was a curiosity to him, a vagabond like himself, who had bulged his way upward. And there the resemblance ceased. The same winds of environment had shaped us differently.

Outwardly he was unmarked. One could not sense in the dainty fellow in evening clothes, a roving pantomimist who had thrown away a fifty cent shirt at the end of each week to save a laundry bill.

While playing as a silent buffoon in a cheap Los Angeles theatre, he was seen by Mack Sennett, an Irish-Canadian then beginning to produce cinema comedies. He was apparently forgotten by Sennett and allowed to wander through the nation buying his weekly fifty cent shirt. Several months later Sennett remembered his antics and decided he had need of him. Chaplin was then in a Pennsylvania town. He was engaged at one hundred and twenty-five dollars a week.

Films were then a crude commodity produced by illiterate men who saddled their taste upon a public which a well known director said was nine years old mentally. The director was not much older.

Perhaps neither Sennett or Chaplin, until their meeting, had ever read a book in their lives. Sennett, whose sense of the ridiculous was broad as a prairie, was an Irishman without emotion, and barren of the nuances of life. In Chaplin, unknowing, he had caught a bird of richer plumage.

Fitted by nature to be a lieutenant of police, or an alderman in an over-populated ward, Mack Sennett, born Michael Sinnott, one time chorus boy and blacksmith, will have a niche in the celluloid mansion of the future for having held the stirrup while the first greatly talented man of the film vaulted into the saddle.

Neither was then, nor ever after, a creative man. Chaplin became, like Sennett, a master of gags—a gag being a remembered incident twisted to fit a situation.

A short while after joining Sennett, the stray little Englishman was the ninth wonder of the comic world.

CHARLIE CHAPLIN

With a new expression and a wider audience—he was soon vastly wealthy.

He was now in the middle of his fame. Though he still wore spats and lived in the pitter-patter of his theatrical world, his chaotic mind was above the average.

Untrained in consecutive thought, and not the conversational equal of several at the table—he was the master of all in mimicry and laughter.

When all were leaving, Chaplin volunteered to take me home in his limousine. Noting my bewilderment in the large car, he laughed and said, "Two beggars, Jim."

As though the mask he had worn all evening had been heavy, he rubbed his eyes.

"I want to see more of you," he said in parting.

A large photograph came to me the next day. It was autographed, "From your fellow comrade, Charlie Chaplin."

Unable to connect the debonair man with the woebegone waif of the screen, I made no further attempt to see him.

Harcourt, my publisher, had given me no advance on the book. The wolf was under the bed. Paul Bern drove him a few hundred feet away. By a ruse and a telegram he convinced Chaplin that I could be useful to him. It was not an important matter to the comedian. My salary of fifty dollars a week would make no dent in his million a year.

When I hesitated, Bern said, "Take a pension from a king when you can."

It was agreed that I was to write articles with Chaplin's name attached, thus adding to my income. He allowed his name to be signed to one article. As sardonic as my master, I remained on the job. If I were less fawning than Boswell, the world famous clown was less sentimental than Johnson—and had far fewer illusions.

Much was to pass between us. Though deference was a mask we both wore, it did not always conceal fierce ego and indomitable pride. I was never to enter fully into his work. He was never to be aware of mine.

"A great artist must have a great audience," he said to me the first week.

"How about Whitman and Nietzsche?" I asked.

They might have been members of a vaudeville team. He made no comment.

Both entirely self-taught, and seeing the worst of life early, we were equally cynical and well trained for the roles assigned to us in life.

My equal in apprehension, he was my superior in the social graces. Reading deeply from childhood, I had absorbed the great minds of the ages. They had come to Chaplin with success, through such men as Max Eastman and Waldo Frank. Though I had written but one book, I was striving to be an artist.

The fairness of a man who analyzes another should

be considered. If at times I make of Chaplin a toy Hamlet in a tinsel town I hope it will be remembered that my compassion and understanding cover much.

His early years wrote with heavy and terrible hand upon him. Though he became their master, and in so doing acquired the manners of a Chesterfield, a remembered sorrow had early turned to gall within him. For what was left of an accidental battle with environment, I had something like respect.

The master simulator of the age, only in anger or solitude was he ever himself. Often childish in quarreling, he was above vengeance.

Imperious and scornful and often attacked with acute melancholia, he would hide such qualities in public. Well meaning people, ever on the alert to evade logic, wished to protect him. Their impulse was wasted. Cesare Borgia was no more able to take care of himself.

Intelligent men seldom impressed him. For H. G. Wells, the son of a servant, he had patronizing tolerance. For Shaw, brittle as glass and as easily seen through, he had more respect.

Like Dickens, he came from the dregs of London. His vision was greater than the novelist's in that he could see futility. With the exception of his work, he was generally devoid of sentimentality or self-pity.

Volatile, turbulent and petulant, his malice died with his anger. He had often the detachment of a first rate man. His charm, his ease of manner, his graciousness, were undeniable. He never made comment on those who had wrongfully used him. Neither did he ever speak of a kindness he had done for another.

He could enjoy intense solitude. For hours, alone, he would thumb the piano and chant broken fragments of pathetic songs.

So abstracted did he become one evening he forgot my presence in the room. The lights of the street followed dusk, and slanted across the good-looking mimic. On the calm water of the spirit, I did not wish to break the spell.

It was near midnight when he asked, "Are you there, Jim?"

When I answered, he said, "Let's take a walk."

Going through the deserted studio, we passed along the dark streets to Hollywood Boulevard.

Moon and stars hung low. He watched them for some moments.

"Napoleon wondered if there wasn't a God, who made those stars," I said.

His gaze left the sky. "One guess is as good as another —a weird man, Napoleon."

"Yes," I volunteered. "On the way to his coronation he said, 'The same people would turn out to see me going to the guillotine'."

The comedian laughed dolefully.

CHARLIE CHAPLIN

There had recently been a sensational execution. The death of a beautiful young woman in England returned to him. Fear of poverty and gossip had made her kill her child. "Come dear," said the hangman, "I'd rather love ye than hang ye."

His face was solemn as we turned on the well lit boulevard.

Brooding for hours at a time, untrained and illogical, the poisoned weeds of a frustrated childhood had grown rank in his mind.

More feminine than masculine in his approach to life, no man better concealed disdain with charm and a lack of trust in all men with unctious, appealing manner, and a smile that would have melted the heart of Cromwell.

Politeness was his house of steel, his bulwark against the rough, never-ending waves that would otherwise have engulfed him.

He was contemptuous of praise. When Fauré, the French author of *The History of Art* went into panegyrics over him, I read the words aloud. Chaplin listened with the expression of one who thought Fauré quite gullible. He did not care for the opinions of Gilbert Seldes, Konrad Bercovici, Max Eastman and other self-appointed midwives of art. Neither did he like contempt. When George Jean Nathan said that if he had genius it was in his sit spot, he smiled forlornly.

Of Elmer Ellsworth, my predecessor, who could laugh

at him while taking his money, he said, "a real highbrow."

The rascal in Frank Harris appealed to him. He was touched by the tragedy of Oscar Wilde. Alone among masters of words, he liked Wilde. The Irishman's chapter on Wainwright, the pioneer, enthralled him. The facile falsity of such sentences as "Like most artificial people, he had a great love of nature," escaped him.

Neither sunset nor star, nor mauve on evening mountain, appealed to him. He once spoke of the London fog, and hoped to die in it. "It draped the buildings and hid their ghastly ugliness."

Inept upon the screen, the helpless foil of invidious circumstance, in private life he was forceful, domineering, arrogant.

A chameleon of the emotions, he was often criticized by radicals who wanted him to be more revolutionary. He smiled with the cynic who said it was presumption in any man to be burned for an opinion—he might be wrong.

His disdain was greater than his pity.

He had the shrewd man's distrust of a lawyer, and horror at all things pertaining to business.

With love for no country, he had none of the duplicity so common in business and politics.

If adroit, it was to protect himself. "My moods are all I have left." They were many and variable. Like beautiful women, they were the problems of his life.

He had no antagonism toward any race or creed. Once

when speaking of Negroes, he said, "I never laugh at their humor. They have suffered too much ever to be funny to me."

"Other races have suffered as much—and with greater sensibilities," I returned.

He remained silent.

He did not believe in large remuneration—for others. His salary list was the lowest in Hollywood.

When Diego Rivera told me that Chaplin had given $50,000 to the Communist cause, I said, "It must have been money of the Madera regime."

Uncomprehending, Rivera did not smile.

He had, however, a generous quality. Edna Purviance, who was his comedy foil for many years, long received two hundred and fifty dollars a week. Her wage with him was never more than that amount, while women of the same ability were earning several thousand weekly. But Edna had not worked in many years.

When he met Granville Redmond, a deaf and dumb artist of more than usual ability, he invited him to make his headquarters at the Chaplin Studio. Redmond remained there until his death. Several of his paintings adorned Chaplin's home.

A mendicant master of legerdemain often entertained him on the London streets. When old and infirm, he wrote the famous clown a letter asking for aid. Chaplin immediately put him on his pension list with the comment, *"He was a very great artist."*

When Mack Swain, the nationally known comedian, incurred the wrath of a movie mogul, and could not obtain employment, Chaplin engaged him at $250.00 per week, telling him that when *The Gold Rush* was finished other companies would pay him much more. They did.

Monta Bell, later a successful director, was one of the most efficient men he ever employed. Feeling that his salary of $150.00 per week was too low, he asked Chaplin for a raise of $50.00 weekly.

Chaplin had but recently released five old films that reverted to him, for a million dollars. Bell did not obtain the raise.

It was Monta Bell who wrote the book about Chaplin's trip to Europe. The comedian's name was attached. It sold less than twenty thousand copies. "There's no money in books," he remarked sagely.

His Japanese valet, Kono, would hand him twenty-five dollars each morning for spending money. He would often have a portion of the money left at night.

No man was allowed to pick up a dinner check at Chaplin's table.

He admired Eleanore Dusé. When she came to Los Angeles, a journalist, Harry Carr, knowing my connection with Chaplin, decided it would be excellent to have the comedian's opinion of the subtle Italian's acting. It fell in with Chaplin's mood. As if studying his arrival, he came late. No one was seated while Dusé was on the stage. We remained in the rear of the theatre. The lights on, we marched down the aisle. Receiving an ovation, for which he was prepared, he bowed in surprised self-consciousness.

Madame Dusé fascinated him. Gesticulating and saying, "Marvelous! Marvelous!" he hurried away at the last curtain, and left me to accompany the journalist and write *his opinion* of the actress.

If he ever read what I had written he made no comment.

He did not again mention Dusé.

He once attempted to write. A London editor asked him for an article on social conditions in America. However little he knew of the subject, it intrigued him. *It was something he would do himself.* He labored valiantly for some time, but could not get his thoughts in order. A few paragraphs of misspelled words were the result. He lost interest.

"How's the article coming, Charlie?" I asked him. He looked at me quizzically and did not reply.

When Eleanor Glyn met him, she said, "Why you don't look nearly as funny as I thought you would."

The madame in the bawdy house of words did not confuse him. His retort was, "Neither do you."

His favorite story was that of Joseph Grimaldi, the

great English-Italian clown, going to a nerve specialist.

"I would recommend that you see Grimaldi," said the doctor.

"*I am Grimaldi,*" was the worn return.

His mansion in Beverly Hills, furnished in flamboyant taste, was architecturally simple as a barn.

He had no vanity about personal apparel and was more careful about his tramp make-up than in dressing for dinner.

He had an aversion for neckwear and for all articles of clothing that hampered the free movement of his body. He often did not shave for several days.

He would walk about the set, his head down, snapping his fingers and talking to himself.

Odd characters alone interested him. But never for long.

It was claimed that fear of weak vocal chords made him refuse to talk upon the screen. This was unjust.

I recall his rehearsing a group in a French song. Mimic-like, he could pronounce the words without knowing their meaning. He would walk across the stage, chanting beautifully, the others following. When they returned, singing without him, something had gone from the group. It was the sublime actor with the rich and resonant voice.

With the exception of stage and screen, his knowledge of all other subjects was superficial.

His reputation brought with it a certain awe. As a result, people listened politely who knew more about the subject of which he was talking than himself.

He seldom glanced at his own publicity.

Fond of the violin, he could evoke certain weird tones from the instrument. Otherwise, he could not play.

Men who considered themselves quite close to him were often mistaken. One such gentleman, who called himself Chaplin's "father confessor," called at the studio.

The comedian looked from a window. Beholding his "father confessor," he made a frantic effort to hide and at last succeeded in getting into a clothes closet. With the usual prevarication, the caller was told that Chaplin would not appear at the studio that day.

In departing, the gentleman said, "Well, just tell Charlie that I dropped in to say 'hello.' "

Perspiring and panting, Charlie emerged from the closet. Being told the visitor's message, he wiped his forehead and exclaimed, "Why the devil didn't he send it on a postal card?"

He took his work seriously. When I slumbered in a story conference of *The Gold Rush* he awakened me with, "Jim, you're a snob." It was one of the few compliments he ever paid me.

His kindness took strange turns. There were two sisters in London whom he knew in childhood. When one wrote of her distress he placed her on a small pension. The other he did not answer.

While dining in Hollywood a well known director came to our table. As we were leaving, Chaplin invited him to the studio. Halfway there Chaplin decided he did not want to see the director. It was my duty to meet him at the gate and explain that Chaplin had been called into an important conference.

Chagrined at Hollywood genius, the director stamped angrily away.

His staff had one device by which to furnish him ideas. No matter how original the thought was, each member would say, "I was just thinking of that gag you told me about, Charlie—it's a good one."

When his assistant director went to New York suddenly without permission and remained a month, all at the studio speculated as to whether or not Chaplin would discharge him. The comedian was silent. When the assistant suddenly appeared on the lot, Chaplin greeted him and said, "Go back to work now and be a good boy."

The assistant was later made a director at another studio. He gave Chaplin two weeks' notice. The comedian was very courteous and told him that it was his duty to better himself.

Five minutes after the assistant had gone Chaplin called his business manager and said, "Fire him at once."

He took no pride when former assistants succeeded

elsewhere. Always when their names were mentioned he had an expression of supercilious contempt.

He would recognize no equal. When he met another great buffoon, W. C. Fields, they chatted amiably. Hours later, Fields recalled that Chaplin did not mention Bill's work upon the screen.

Walking with him along a side street in Hollywood, we passed a house in front of which a wedding party was being photographed. Observing Chaplin, the group called to him. He consented to be photographed with the bride and groom.

He held his head down for some minutes after we had gone. Finally he said, "Poor devils."

The talk drifted to children. He recalled his baby that died at birth. It had been called "The Little Mouse" by its mother, Mildred Harris, who was his first wife.

His eyes narrowed. "The undertaker put a little prop smile on its face." He stopped a second. "You know, Jim, that kid never smiled."

Lita Grey was engaged during my period with him. If five minutes lost the battle of Waterloo, it was enough to create havoc in the comedian's life. He was selecting a girl to play opposite him in *The Gold Rush*. He wanted one who was unknown. Names meant money. Many beautiful and talented young women appeared and did their pathetic best before the camera. Their work was seen by the great buffoon in the projection room.

None pleased his sardonic majesty. At last Lita Grey appeared at the studio. She was living with her Mexican mother and grandparents in a small bungalow nearby. Very poor, her bumptious animal life and beauty, blended of the hoyden, were her chief attributes, making the beholder forget her tawdry apparel in the glory of her awakening womanhood. She was about sixteen, bold as a pirate and carefree as the wind. Black eyes, black hair and a round face, she had neither sensibility, poise nor thought. Backward in school, she could not be forced to study. The Board of Education pursued her with its truant officers and teachers until she was eighteen, and then retreated.

When told that Chaplin was not at the studio, she said, "I'll wait five minutes."

Any other day but the one upon which his destiny was written he might not have appeared at the studio at all. He now came within the five minutes.

Lita had worked with him in a film some years before. About twelve then, she remained in Chaplin's mind.

He greeted her with enthusiasm and ordered a camera test of her at once.

Foregoing lunch, we waited to see it upon the screen. Though she had less acting ability than any girl who had applied, Chaplin began to say, "Marvelous! Marvelous!" Seated next to him, and not wishing to endanger my already insecure position by being too direct and honest, I went to my office.

Aloof from the other stooges, I was seldom consulted by him. By some cantankerous whim, he left them at the projection room door, and followed me.

"What do you think of her, Jim?" he asked.

Evading, I asked in return, "What do you think of her, Charlie?"

"Marvelous, marvelous," was the answer.

He walked up and down the room hurriedly.

Lita Grey entered. "Did you like the test, Charlie?" she shouted.

He became cautious. "Not bad, not bad." Admiration conquered cupidity. "You're engaged," he said, laughing.

She jumped up and down, clapping her hands and exclaiming, "Goody, goody."

A contract was prepared, a photograph taken of her signing.

"Don't look at your salary," he laughed.

He had engaged a leading lady at $75.00 a week.

They were soon everywhere together.

During the height of his romance, he asked my opinion of her.

I was frank, and answered, "A young animal—nothing else."

He studied. "I know. I was teasing her last night. She admitted she might like me better because I'm Charlie Chaplin." His eyes became weary. "If I were a clerk, she would not want me."

"Would you blame her, Charlie—all the moods of Lord Byron in a clerk."

"But women loved Lord Byron."

"Not as a clerk."

"Oh, well—it makes no difference," he said.

After their marriage in Mexico, remembering, no doubt, my opinion of his wife, he still avoided me.

Months passed.

Except for a love of play, his child wife had nothing in common with him. There were chords in the great comedian that echoed to grander music. The weary and life-hurt man in search of something his intelligence might have told him he never would find, was soon in the bogs of disillusion.

An order came to me, "You are to see the prize fights with the boss tonight." My economic law, it had to be obeyed.

For months we had not spoken. It was not considered unusual. Others had often been treated in the same manner. A group of strays from the far and rough fields of the world, we pointed no finger at another in the bad graces of the master. Like the rain, his mantle of disdain fell on all alike.

We dared not express sympathy or give other evidence

of understanding. He abhorred sentimentality, and could not differentiate.

I joined him that evening.

The past was not mentioned.

We talked of the ring and the workings of the mind as connected with pugilists. Chaplin closed his eyes when a stout-hearted bruiser went to the canvas. "Terrible! Terrible!"

The last round ended, people clustered about him. Smiling, as always, in public, he hurried away with me.

For hours his chauffeur drove along the Pacific.

We arrived at his Beverly Hills mansion before dawn.

It was many weeks before he talked to me again.

He parted and soon settled with Lita Grey. With hardly a change of clothing a short time before, she now had an immense fortune.

He had never been able to teach her to act. Neither were the best artists of the camera capable of making her photograph well.

A superb ironist, he knew when to laugh at himself.

While on location in Nevada for *The Gold Rush,* five hundred vagabonds greeted him. Selected to make the trek over Chilcoot Pass, they were blue with cold.

"They are cheering for you, Charlie," I said.

"I know." His eyes were slightly disdainful under the battered derby. "How'd you like to be back among them?"

A DOZEN AND ONE

"It could be worse," was my answer.

He shrugged his shoulders in his tight-fitting tramp coat. "I'd rather be me than them."

On our journey to Hollywood he called on a noted editor in Sacramento. A heavy featured, red faced and aging, matter-of-fact man, the editor might have been talking to an elf. Before one who could write an editorial about the price of beets or the abdication of an emperor, Chaplin smiled charmingly and said, Yes, yes, yes," or "Marvelous, marvelous." At last he excused himself. On the street he frowned and said, "Lord—what a man!"

His most humiliating love affair was with Pola Negri. That tempestuous female treated him worse than the others. His chagrin was deep when he thought another had supplanted him. "That ham actor," he said in disgust.

He could be amazingly kind and understanding in those rare moments when the cynical curtains of his soul were parted.

His intuition, rated highly in Hollywood, was not always accurate. I was once at his mansion with Harry D'Arrast, a Basque nobleman then serving the King of Laughter. Worried about my own future, I listened patiently to the nothings uttered by nobleman and king.

Chaplin decided suddenly that the three of us would go to the beach.

He ran upstairs.

Knowing that such a jaunt would last until early

morning, I exclaimed in despair, "I'm going to tell him I'm through—I've had enough of this—I'd rather starve."

The nobleman put his arm about me. "Brace up, Jim," he consoled. "We're both prostitutes."

Returning, Chaplin saw the pain in my eyes.

"Don't take the picture too seriously, Jim," he said.

His mind went, laughing, to other and lighter things.

He had learned the use of more or less correct English by a "good ear" and observation.

Hearing the word "apropos," from Monta Bell, he inquired the definition. Everything was "apropos" with him for some time.

Not physically brave, he was a tyrant toward his half brother, Sydney. Without Charlie's capacity, Sydney remained a varnished cockney. Unlike the more Oriental Charlie, he was of light complexion, with slick hair parted in the middle, and the manner of a promoted bank clerk.

He had told a journalist that in childhood he and Charlie were forced to live on thrown-away food.

As Charlie was at that time trying to establish his birth as in aristocratic Fontainebleau, France, an article by the journalist upset him. He sent for Sydney, and heaped vituperation upon him until his rage was exhausted. When Sydney left in silence, Chaplin pounded the piano and scraped the violin. His mood did not lift for the rest of the evening.

The only man who ever received a large salary from

him was Adolphe Menjou. The comedian was dining with Peggy Joyce when Menjou entered the restaurant.

"There's the leading man for *A Woman of Paris*." said Peggy.

Menjou was asked to call at the studio. After weeks of dickering, he was engaged at $500.00 per week.

Menjou, French and Irish, with military and college training, "stole" the film and became a star.

A tawdry story, it was saved by his acting.

Coming in a year of bad films, it was lauded highly by those who should have been more discriminating. Their comments filled newspapers and magazines until even Chaplin grew weary.

He was fond of animals, and might, in a mood, have stopped his limousine to be kind to a stray dog.

The canine that played with him in *A Dog's Life* remained a pet at the studio until the end of his decrepit days. He lived with the watchman at the front gate. Whenever the comedian appeared, the dog would follow him. This pleased Chaplin more than the plaudits of the great.

He made peaceful the last years of his mother's life, and often discussed her. He was proud of her ability as an actress. "They can say what they want about her," he said, "She was a greater artist than I will ever be. She *was* a great actress. I've never seen anyone like her. She was good to me when I was a kid. She gave me all she had and asked nothing in return—and I've got no mother complex either."

There was about her a handsome, gypsy-like quality that Chaplin inherited. He would look at her with a tinge of sadness. Without being tender, he was deferential to her. She called him "The King."

There were lines in her face of a woman who had suffered much. More sedate than her son, she was austere and proud, with the look in her eyes of one who could not bow to life, but must face it erect to the last.

She had long suffered recurrent attacks of mental illness undoubtedly caused by the vicissitudes of worry and extreme poverty. Less complex than her mental-torn son, she retained the religion of her childhood.

When government flunkies tried to deport her to the England of her early suffering, Chaplin fought valiantly to have her remain near him in California. There was in him concerning her, as with all the insoluble things in life, a sense of wonder that reached at times the pinnacle of terror.

Nowhere in Zola is there a story equal to hers.

"They used to let her go when they thought her mind was well," her talented son said. "In a few hours she'd find a place to live, get someone to trust her for material to make sacks, and by night she'd have a dozen ready to sell . . . and the first thing she'd do was get Syd and me. I'll never forget that.

A DOZEN AND ONE

"One time we came home and found her gone. We thought the worst but hoped we were wrong. It's not so easy for a kid to come home and find his mother taken away. So we knocked at the doors of all the rooms to find someone who could tell us something. At last a big woman opened a door and we asked a lot of questions. She couldn't tell us a thing. She was deaf and dumb.

"They had taken her away again. I'd visit her each week. The guard would let me take her out under a tree. Many a time I couldn't talk for an hour afterward."

Of his father, Chaplin spoke but seldom. A music hall entertainer and a dandy in his day, he was blown by the winds of theatrical circumstance around London and vanished early. Tales are told of him, mostly legend. It is likely that he inherited an Oriental, Latin, or Jewish strain from his father.

He ridiculed sentimentality too often in others not to have had a touch of it himself.

The publishers of Thomas Burke's *The Wind and The Rain* sent him a copy of that book. Secluded in a bungalow at the far end of the studio, oblivious of everything else, he read and discussed it at great length, saying, "It's my Bible."

"Charlie," I suggested, "it would be a nice thing to send Burke's publishers a boost for the book."

"Write it. I'll send it." He did.

Long afterward, Burke requested a photograph. I

brought one for his signature. Chaplin looked at it. "It's not good enough," he said.

In London, four years later, I asked Burke if he had ever received the photograph.

"Not yet," he answered.

One evening at dusk Burke had wandered through the streets of the London East End with Chaplin.

Each full of his own bitter youthful years in that section, the two famous walkers were silent for several blocks. They then stood in an open hallway and watched a group of children playing under the glare of a yellow light across the street.

Burke finally said, "Charlie, if you want to do something fine—go over and tell those children that you're Charlie Chaplin."

The comedian shook his head, saying, "I don't like children."

They walked away in silence.

He did not drink liquor, and seldom smoked a cigarette. His energy was enormous. His physical condition excellent, he could run a far distance without tiring. In company he was dainty at table.

Restless as a storm, his mind was always active.

All things pathological interested him. The Leopold-Loeb case held his attention for months. He had something akin to pity for the Chicago anarchists executed after the Haymarket riot.

An hour before his doom, one brave fellow sang:
"Maxwelton braes are bonnie,
Where early fa's the dew—
It was there that Annie Laurie
Gae me her promise true."

He would shake his head slowly in memory of the incident.

Suddenly growing tired of others, he again desired my company. I was to go with him to dinner.

"He's in a dark mood," a co-worker said. Sensing tedious hours ahead, I looked about for help.

On an errand in Hollywood, I met a young woman of whom he was fond. Experience had taught me that if she should "accidentally" come into the Montmartre, where we were to have dinner, he would invite her to remain and send me home. I asked her to come to the restaurant, and to make it appear accidental.

As we went toward his accustomed table, he stopped suddenly. There sat the two men of whom he was tired.

He turned angrily about, saying, "I've got no privacy at all," and hurried out of the restaurnat. We went to another cafe. It was crowded.

His chauffeur followed us in the car.

He then decided to go to the Ambassador Hotel. Once there, we remained at the same table for more than five hours.

I was completely talked out.

CHARLIE CHAPLIN

In silence, Chaplin watched the dancers. A Spanish girl began to flirt with him. *Hope rose again.* If she would only come to his table, *he might excuse me.* I praised her beauty. The comedian watched her. In desperation, I said, "Why don't you chat with her, Charlie? She's very lovely."

He answered, "I'm not in the mood, Jim. It's lovelier just to watch her."

The young woman arrived at the Montmartre as planned. The two men were still at the table. *We* had come—and *gone.*

He was not always considerate of romantic young ladies. At a swimming club, it seemed that nothing would happen to break the monotony of our companionship. A woman asked if she might meet the great Mr. Chaplin. A very beautiful young girl of sixteen was with her. Introductions over, we chatted until Chaplin invited them to dine with us.

The girl, who had graduated from high school at fifteen, was attending an exclusive finishing school. She was the comedian's match in clever repartee. He was much taken with her. I watched the proceedings with entire satisfaction. *He might send me home.*

The dinner over, Chaplin asked the young lady to call at the studio next day.

On the way to Beverly Hills, I expatiated upon the girl's charm, her beauty, and clever mind.

He leaned back in the limousine with a rapt expression. He agreed with me volubly. I was pleased.

The girl called at the studio. He refused to see her.

Our roads diverged after eighteen months, through no fault of Chaplin's.

His manager, Al Reeves, a fine gentleman, had given me my choice of removing a sardonic line I had written about Chaplin in a then unpublished manuscript, or being discharged.

I chose the latter.

We did not part in anger, but indifference.

A week later, the remaining stooges had dinner with him. All but Charles Reisner, an ex-bruiser like myself, and now a successful director, put me on the griddle. When all was over, and the last feather in my soul had been plucked by the stooges, Chaplin still gazing at his water glass, said slowly, "Well—he deserves a lot of credit."

He later included me and the owners and editors of a national magazine in a damage suit for a half million dollars. To illustrate the life story I had sold them, the editors had used his photograph . . . without his consent. As there was evidently a law in the state of New York against such procedure, the great comedian, or his lawyer, immediately considered themselves damaged to this enormous amount.

As the editors of the magazine, valiant in the service

of their readers, whom they said, were mostly women and children, had told me that I could say no word that would destroy their idol, and as lawyers from each side had gone over the "copy" there could be no libel. It was the only thing left upon which to base a suit.

The editors had also requested that I write Chaplin, inform him of my plan, and tell him very gently that I would in no way injure him. This I did. He did not reply.

The deal had been made at the Harvard Club. I smile in memory at one vagabond selling the life of another while dead presidents of that institution of snobbery, enshrined in the oil of oblivion, looked from the walls.

I did not tell the editors what I considered the real cause of the suit. The comedian, like all inarticulate men, had an ambition to write. Some day he would sell the story of his life for a hundred and fifty, perhaps two hundred thousand dollars.

I thought I did very well at the Harvard Club, and not being a parlour socialist, was satisfied.

There was vast worry. One editor told me that a monthly issue of the magazine, if one were foolish enough to pile one copy on another, would reach higher toward the clouds than any building in New York.

The great day came. Nathan Burkan and his aides lined up for their mightily damaged client. The attorneys for the magazine were in array against them.

I would not dare to quote the judge, whose name was

Thatcher, and whose views as I heard of them, were sensible. Inasmuch as Chaplin had become world famous and wealthy by the use of his photograph, it was no time to object. He dismissed the case in less than a half hour.

Years later, Chaplin wrote the story of his life for another magazine.

I met him socially while the legal squabble was in progress. While working on a play with the husband of a socially ambitious wife, I was invited to a party. When I arrived the lady told me that Mr. Chaplin was coming. Miss Marion Davies had telephoned late that afternoon, requesting that she be allowed to bring him. Realizing that such a social lion as the mimic was hard to capture, I accepted the inevitable.

He arrived, urbane as usual. The shrewd showman would allow no ex-hobo to steal a situation from him. He even seemed to be glad I was there.

"Why, hello, Jim. I've wanted so much to talk to you," he said, looking about at the cinema butterflies.

At that moment we were friends. When a charade was played, he selected me to assist him. It was suggested that we play a word with four syllables. He laughed and said, "Lord, I don't know any."

He invited me to get in touch with him next day. I did not do so. His mood might have changed.

Long after, at dusk, I stood in a hallway on Sunset

CHARLIE CHAPLIN

Boulevard. A man came toward me. His hands were buried deep in his pockets. His cap was pulled low over his eyes. His shoulders slumped, as though the world were upon them. He did not look up, but passed, silent as a shadow on a screen, into the darkness. It was Charlie Chaplin, the most popular man on earth.

I had an impulse to say, "Hello, Charlie," and then refrained. I have been sorry since.

He was in the mood I liked best—that of the frustrated fellow without his mask, who had reached for a star and had pulled down a dusty apple.

CLARK GABLE

CLARK GABLE

A miracle among actors, he has surpassed Rudolph Valentino's popularity.

Now in middle life, he resembles Jack Dempsey in physique and contour of head and face. He has also the power and gentleness of the great bruiser.

Clark Gable comes of Pennsylvania Dutch stock. One would hardly expect such a fellow to become a volatile and powerful actor. I feel now, as I did at the beginning of his screen career, that he will continue to develop for a great many years to come.

Like Dempsey, his roots go down deep into life. He is great enough to be simple. Having walked with hunger, it has left him poised and unafraid. Again like Dempsey, he is the least belligerent of men. But nevertheless, there is iron under the velvet of Gable.

I have seen him put a twenty dollar note in the hand of a hungry extra girl, and his hand over her mouth when she tried to thank him. He knows the tawdry answers of poverty.

He was born in a small Ohio town, the son of a contractor and a lovely girl who died when he was seven months old. He still has a few faded water colors she painted in her girlhood.

His maternal grandparents took him "to raise." One of his earliest recollections is that of gazing from the kitchen window of the farm house at a hen lost in a blinding snow storm. His grandmother stood over a wood

stove making tomato ketchup. He drew attention to the
hen. His grandmother took the ketchup from the stove
and rescued it. To this day, the odor of cooking tomatoes
makes him homesick.

From his grandmother he learned the principles of
living that have guided him ever since; that there can
be no harvest without first tilling the soil and sowing the
seed; that life is a great adventure on a far and winding
road, and that a smile is always welcome even when the
heart is sad.

The farm house faced Coneaut Lake. There were no
other houses near, so the first six years of Clark's life
were solitary and character building. He swam in the
lake, watched squirrels in the hickory grove and buzzards
wheel above in the far blue sky. Each Sunday the old
mare was hitched to the surrey and he accompanied
his grandparents to church.

When his father married again he came after the
boy. There were tearful farewells. It can still be recorded
that his grandparents remained in his life.

When Clark reached home he found his step-parent
a kindly woman who treated him as if she were his own
mother.

Hopedale, the Ohio village in which his father lived,
contained five hundred people. To the solitary little boy,
it was a vast city. As is his nature, he soon made friends
with everybody in the town. An accident in his childhood

brought him into contact with a bluff village doctor. For some years he decided to study medicine.

The solitary life with his grandparents had influenced him a great deal. All through high school the future great matinee idol was bashful in the presence of girls. After graduating he went to Akron, Ohio, with the hope of working his way through medical school. He was seventeen and had never been in so large a city before. Afraid to venture into the city alone, he remained in the railroad station for several hours.

At last he went forth and rented a cheap room. He spent some time in writing letters to his stepmother and his grandparents. More courage came with the morning and he went to a large rubber factory in search of work. As the factory employed ten thousand people, there were several hundred men in line. He secured work as a time keeper.

He immediately enrolled in the pre-medic class and attended the night school of the University of Akron. His routine was the same for many months. Five nights a week he went to school. The other two evenings were for rest and diversion.

There was in the factory at the time a young actor named Eddie Grisdale down on his luck. He struck up a friendship with Clark and by a sheer accident changed the course of his life. Thinking there was a mistake of several hours in his time, when he was quitting his job

47

at the factory, the actor went to young Gable to have it rectified.

He said to Gable, "Why don't you come and see me act? I'll take you back of the wings."

"Sure, I will, Eddie." They shook hands and the time-keeper, busy with his work, thought no more of the incident until the following Saturday night.

Then he called on his friend. The young actor let him look through the peep hole of the curtain. For the first time he saw the sea of expectant faces beyond. His life was changed. He knew he would never be a doctor.

He never again attended night school but went to the theater each night. The manager made him a call boy— without salary. After a month he was given a lineless part and actually walked upon the stage without fear. He learned the tricks of make-up from different members of the company. Six more weeks passed and the overjoyed boy was given a speaking part. A butler, he bowed and said, "Good evening, Madam."

After nearly a year, he played small rôles with success. While in the most difficult part he had portrayed, he was given the news of his stepmother's death. Saying no word to any member of the company, he played the rôle.

The next morning he went to console his father and remained at home for a month. When the elder Gable, still feeling his loss, decided to leave Ohio for the oil fields of Oklahoma, Clark dutifully accompanied him. For over a year he worked in the fields from dawn to dark. With the dust of the stage still in his lungs, the grimy and greasy work did not appeal to him. So he left his father and joined a little traveling theatrical company in Kansas City. It played in churches, barns, theatres, wherever possible in all the western states.

The young actor was happy. It was for him the rainbow in a murky sky—the satisfaction of his soul.

At last, to make the history of such adventures complete, the company was stranded in Butte, Montana. Gable counted his assets on a bitterly cold morning. He had two dimes, a nickel, a penny, and a heart without fear. He would go forward—no matter where, or how.

One of the ironical whimsies of life is that would-be actors must eat. Clark wandered about Butte until all but five cents had gone for food. Then weary with walking, he slept "sitting up" in the waiting room of the depot until dawn. His five cents would get him "coffee and rolls." Beyond that! well what does it matter when one is young and wants to be an actor?

He went to the wash room to douse the sleep from his eyes. A genial dark nuisance began to brush his clothes. He whisked the broom so affectionately about poor Clark's neck, that the future screen star gave him his one and only nickel.

Even with money one can be very lonely and blue in

the heart of any city. Butte was no different. It is, however, in the parlance of the road, "a good town." So Clark
Gable, hands in his pockets, and eyes unseeing the golden
road ahead, heard his hungry footsteps echo on the
empty street.

His mind was made up. He would go to Portland,
Oregon. Friends from Ohio lived in that city. It was
hundreds of miles away, and he did not have a cent.
Even Napoleon, broke in Butte, might indulge in self
pity. So did Clark for a moment. Finally he said to himself, "Oh, well, no one asked me to be an actor." It was
an admirable thought. But coffee and doughnuts were
still far away.

Standing in front of a well lit all night restaurant, he
saw a man approaching. His walk was between a shamble
and a stagger. He was gloriously inebriated, and singing
loudly—

> *"Once loved a woman,*
> *That came to an end,*
> *Get a good dog, boys—*
> *He's always your friend."*

Clark grinned at the weaving man.

"You look hungry, bo," the man hiccoughed.

"How did you guess?" asked Clark.

"Oh, I know," returned the drunken psychologist,
"everybody looks hungry in this damn town." He swayed
before the restaurant door. "Come on in," he said. Still

shambling, with Clark following, he yelled, "Two orders of ham and eggs." Then the eternal question of the road, "Which way, bo?"

And Clark answered, "Portland."

"That's me—I'm headin' that way—quick as I get sober."

"And I'm beatin' it too—I wouldn't pay a railroad a cent if I was richer'n Rockefeller—no, sir—they get no dough from Jack Bates—I got to have money to drink on."

Beautiful as dawn the ham and eggs were spread before Gable. Then by a peculiar quirk of the inebriated, Jack Bates decided that ham and eggs were not what he wanted at all.

"Leave them here—that's all right," Mr. Gable said to the waiter. "I don't want to see them go to waste."

That night they were on a freight train.

"Take this," said Jack Bates, "so if we get separated you'll have eatin' money." He handed Clark five dollars.

They remained together for several days and then became separated. Clark's money was gone when he reached Portland.

"It was quite a walk," to where his friends lived. He eventually got there to find they had left for Ohio the day before. Disconsolate, he was given lodging at the Salvation Army Hotel. He ate sparingly until a troupe of players appeared for three days at a Portland theatre, and left for Astoria. This made no impression in Oregon whatever; but Clark Gable was with them. He was jubilant. The manager had explained that his was a profit sharing company. In fourteen performances Clark's share of the profits was two dollars.

In desperation, he went to a general employment agency and obtained a job with a party of engineers leaving to survey forest tracts in Southern Oregon. He worked as a rod man for several months, plodding through the heavy forest country, bitten by insects, and poisoned by shrubbery. Each day it rained. His clothes were never completely dry.

He then drew all his money and went back to Portland. His next job was in the "help wanted" department of a newspaper. He would see an advertisement for a good job first. After two months of watching, he discovered that the local telephone company had advertised for a personable young man with opportunity for advancement. It was an office position. Clark remained a year before another violent attack of stage fever brought him down. This time, with two hundred dollars saved, he went to Hollywood.

For months he loitered about the studios without obtaining work. His money was gone, his position hopeless, when one morning he stood in a group of men from which twelve of the tallest were selected. Gable was among them. For a week he stood motionless in the tight fitting suit of a grenadier on an Ernest Lubitsch set. Each night he received seven dollars and fifty cents. Once the great Lubitsch looked at him casually. Gable's heart nearly stopped.

That hit or miss method of living went on for months. He averaged one day a week as an extra player.

When Louis MacLoon produced *Romeo and Juliet* on the stage with Jane Cowl as the star, a tall soldier was needed to carry a spear. Clark was chosen. At last he was in a metropolitan theatre. The spear was light as a feather. So was his heart.

Though millions of women now worship the fellow who gave his last nickel to a colored porter, it was Jane Cowl who first held out a dainty hand to him. Through her influence he was given a small speaking part as a *comedy soldier*. When later, MacLoon produced *What Price Glory*, Gable understudied the actor who played Sergeant Quirt. When he left the company the dynamic Gable stepped in. Now for the first time the throttled spirit of the man broke out. The seasoned MacLoon watched him from the wings. He came to the likeable Ohioan at the end of the play and with emotion said, "You'll do, my boy."

The strain of the long struggle partly over, Gable was ill through the night.

After fifteen weeks, he joined Lionel Barrymore in *The Copperhead*. That splendid actor became his friend.

Part followed part, with lapse of hardship merging on hunger, in between. He landed the role opposite Nancy Carroll in *Chicago*.

Nancy stepped into a successful film carreer, and Gable went to Houston, Texas, as "second man and heavy." In twelve weeks he became the leading man at two hundred dollars a week. He remained seven months.

Then came New York and the leading rôle in *Machinal*.

At the end of the theatrical season he received a wire from his old friend, Louis MacLoon—Would he play Killer Mears in the Los Angeles production of *The Last Mile?*

Who that saw him in that rôle, can ever forget his tremendous portrayal! Vital, tigerish, terrifying, the stage rocked under him.

Still under the torrent turned loose by Gable, Lionel Barrymore said, "Make no mistake about this lad. He has the fire of a wild stallion."

"I won't." I said humbly, having seen the mountain of emotion crack.

John Barrymore joined us. "We've seen something to-night," he said, as we went to Gable's dressing room.

The two great artists, having lived through many such scenes, looked at Gable in silence.

Finally John said, "You're going far, Clark."

"John's wrong," said Lionel. "You're already there."

CLARK GABLE

The rest is a brilliant and vital page in the history of the screen.

"You've had a great success, Clark," I recently said to him. "What would you rather do now more than anything else in the world?"

"Find Jack Bates, Jim," was the quick answer.

Gable was married to Carole Lombard but a short time when her tragic death in an airplane accident shocked the nation. The country boy who became a great matinée idol has never been the same.

Miss Lombard was returning from a bond selling campaign in behalf of the government, when her plane went down but a few hours ride from her husband who awaited her at their home in the San Fernando Valley.

A fellow comrade on all his journeys into the wilds, her sudden passing made him desolate. Unable to stand before a camera at his studio, he joined the Army, thus giving up a salary of seventy five hundred dollars a week, for fifty dollars a month. "If the nation goes, there will be no salaries—and I prefer the nation."

JACK DEMPSEY

JACK DEMPSEY

His forehead slopes. His ears are close to his head. Since the mauling was always too severe "in close to Dempsey," they are not distorted as are the average bruiser's. His eyes are small and vivid. Inside the ropes, they slanted, snake-like, into a steady stare.

His body springs upward as he walks, as though his heels were of highly resilient rubber. His muscles are loose, without bulge. Like a tiger, born the ferocious fighter, he is not muscle-bound.

When he moves quickly, which is often, his feet turn slightly inward and his knees rub together, a habit which he no doubt learned in the ring, to better balance himself under the blows of an adversary.

In conversation, he never directly challenges a statement. He says, "You may be right," or, if in some doubt, "I don't know about that."

He never says yes or no with emphasis.

He loves laughter, gayety, noise, the blare of the band, the climax of a melodrama, the touch of women.

Long trained in sinful valleys, he does not classify men and women according to their morals.

He is of Indian, Irish, Scotch, and Jewish blood. He is contented outdoors so long as there are animals around. As a boy, he would gather in all the stray dogs of the neighborhood.

Unlike most primitive men, he is not religious in the midst of overwhelming forces. Of deep compassion toward all who suffer in the less subtle ways that he can understand, he is without sentimentality. Too honest to pretend, the flattery of fools could never induce him to become pretentious.

He has amused tolerance for the vagaries of others. When writers on sports, who had heard of Shakespeare, spoke of Tunney's love of him, Dempsey smiled and said, "The old boy's all right if he helps Gene's racket."

He has no racial prejudices.

He will not talk of death.

When I told him of Ernie Schaaf's end, after the fight with Carnera, he frowned for a second and said, "Too bad—he was a good boy too," and resumed serving drinks to a group of friends.

His relatives and close friends still call him Champ. He smokes many cigars, and seldom drinks anything intoxicating. His favorite beverage is beer, which he drinks slowly.

He is never without many half-dollar pieces in his pockets. A target for beggars, none are ever refused. A silver coin is flipped casually to all who ask.

Relatives in need have become hesitant about asking for even a small amount of money. Instead of the requested five dollars, he will urge fifty upon them.

If a friend admires a scarf, kerchief, or watch which he wears, he will press it upon him. If he purchases an article for himself, he will do the same for the friend who accompanies him.

Constantly meeting thousands of people, he never forgets a face nor the associations which surround it.

He has earned approximately five million dollars. Of this amount, one woman, a former wife of his, has, perhaps received a million, attorneys another million. Neither by word or manner has he shown any bitterness toward these people.

He is capable of sardonic humor. When, upon being introduced to a judge, I refused to shake hands with him on the ground that he carried a rope, Dempsey did likewise. The legal gentleman, slightly inebriated, appealed to Jack in vain. Roars came from the crowd, all men who had faced judges.

When the judge at last allowed himself to be searched and an amateur magician pulled a rope from his hip pocket, Dempsey was loudest in the laughter.

His mind is the fastest I have ever known among pugilists. Once, at a game of Murder, he was chosen as the prosecutor. His part was to leave the room while the murder was committed.

Upon returning, he was to ask all present to tell what happened and thus find the culprit.

He detected the supposed murderess out of a group of twenty. His questions were so swift and direct that she broke down.

He is able to glance from the ring at an audience and guess within a few hundred dollars how much is in the house.

During his last exhibition tour he signed no contract to appear for less than five thousand dollars.

He is popular with women. A product of a world in which one class of females predominated, he is without illusion concerning the others.

He greets all classes of them with the same friendliness. A habit dating from the days when food was rare, he has often greeted me with, "Did you eat yet?" the common salutation of road-kids.

He has the gentleness of strength conscious of itself. It would nevertheless be dangerous to place a man of eighty in the ring with him.

When an ancient fighter collapsed under his blows in a training-camp, I said to him, "That's too bad." His retort was, "When you get between the ropes you're supposed to take it."

He went to the battered bruiser and asked, "Are you all right?" The fighter's head hung as if his neck were broken. He mumbled, "Yes, Jack."

"That's the stuff," Dempsey patted his shoulder and left.

I turned to look at the fighter, while Dempsey said:

"I learned my lesson early in the game—against Bill Brennan, a nice fellow and a good fighter. I liked him and wanted to let him stick around a while to give him a break, and the crowd a run for its money. He caught me in the third round with a right to the jaw that made me half unconscious. I didn't know a thing until the twelfth round, when I came to and knocked him out. I made up my mind to finish 'em quick after that."

It was really as difficult for Dempsey to pull a punch as for a panther to refrain from leaping at its prey. But he was always ready to help a beaten adversary to his corner.

He can't be made to discuss his kindness toward others, nor their unkindness toward him.

His energy is tireless, relentless. Unless in sleep, he never relaxes. He seldom remains seated for more than a few minutes. Even then, his eyes dart about, his hands move constantly.

On first entering a hotel room, he places a deck of cards at his bedside as carefully as a Christian travelling salesman does a Gideon Bible. He plays solitaire until sleep lulls his restless brain.

Except when in deep distress, his temperament is even, cheerful.

He does not like to drive an automobile. "You can't think at the wheel of the damned thing."

A secretary generally drives his car. When alone, Dempsey sits in the front seat, with a cigar in his mouth. If accompanied by a friend, he huddles in a corner of the rear seat, nervously chewing, but seldom smoking his cigar. At such times his eyes are narrow, his forehead heavily wrinkled.

When he gives an order, the secretary says in a respectful tone, "All right, Champ."

His car was in California in the dead of Winter recently. One day he threw his luggage in the rear and said to the secretary, "We're going to New York, Kid." Through snow and zero weather he was there in ten days.

No physical hardship exists for him.

The career of a politician was spoiled when he entered the ring. He has courage without belligerence, and tact without deceit.

He is at his best in fast conversation.

I listened with him to the Schmeling-Stribling fight returns. As each blow was recorded, his shoulders moved. Reporters crowded about him when the fight was over. Dozens of questions were fired at him. He parried them all.

In a nefarious business, his sense of honor is high.

When I criticized him harshly in a magazine some years ago, he said, "You were hard on me, Jim; but I wasn't so easy on Willard. We've both got places to go."

Though several of his friends came belligerently to his defense, the article was never again mentioned between us.

The pugilist's mother, beyond seventy, is the passion

of his life. After each of his important fights, all of which were held more than two thousand miles away, he would go to her within a week.

Her son inherits her nervous vitality and energy. He never discusses her. There is hardly any open sign of affection between them; at most he will pat her shoulder casually, or kiss, half-bashfully and suddenly, the graying hair on her temple. He plays cards with her when they are alone. On all his transcontinental journeys, which are at least a dozen a year, he stops in Utah to visit her.

When he fought Willard for the championship in Toledo, his young sister, Elsie, played "Beautiful Ohio" on her violin while waiting at home to hear the result.

The telephone rang.

"Well, Mother, I won," said Dempsey's far-away voice. "See you soon."

This brief conversation ended, the mother of the new champion seated herself at an oil-cloth covered table, where she remained, in silence, a long time.

She was disturbed. Jack had been fighting ten years. Her oldest son had also been a pugilist. She had observed fighters who came to the house. In the first hot flush of her son's victory, she thought of his possible end.

The millions that followed left her the same. She would not live in a Hollywood mansion. A small ranch, in sight of the Wasatch mountains, is now her home.

So terrible was the punishment given to Willard, that even his trainers were horror-stricken.

With eyes nearly closed, the face swollen beyond recognition, he stumbled to his dressing room, moaning, "God! God! Oh, God, my God!" He fell on his cot, and turned his battered body in agony to the wall.

His seconds looked at him mutely. Finally, one said, "Come on, Jess, it's all over."

The defeated champion sobbed. He had lost a world. It was all he had.

Before he was dressed, Dempsey came into the room.

His cap, road-kid fashion, was pulled low over his eyes. His arm went around his antagonist. "Never mind, Jess," he consoled, "it's all in the game. We couldn't both win."

Willard moaned, without venom, through inch-thick lips, "Thanks, Jack."

Dempsey smiled. "That's the spirit, Jess—there's a lot of good fights left in you yet," and went on his troubled way.

Willard crumpled before an avalanche of blows delivered with thudding accuracy. Kid McCoy commented after the fight, "I couldn't have lasted five rounds in front of Dempsey the way he fought today."

James J. Corbett once told me that Sullivan was a harder puncher than Dempsey, but this was only ego in defense of itself. Corbett had never fought Dempsey.

Neither had Sullivan ever knocked out such a man as Carl Morris with one blow under the heart, nor had he ever battered to defeat three such men as Willard, Firpo, and Carpentier, in less than ten rounds each.

But it is true, as Corbett contended, that Sullivan knocked out more men in one tour than Dempsey has in all his life.

The old-time fighters and their managers resorted to many tricks to save the thousand dollars they offered to any man who stayed four rounds. The manager of the touring gladiator always held the watch. If his man tired, the round was shortened, but if the gentleman seeking to earn the thousand became tired, the round was lengthened.

At a certain time in the exhibition he was backed against the curtain of the theatre, and the touring gladiator would knock his head against the curtain at the exact second a mallet struck it from the other side.

Thus the money would be saved and a knockout would be recorded for the bruiser on tour.

Both Sullivan and Corbett were well aware of such tricks.

Dempsey was promoter and referee of a fight in Reno several years ago. When the preliminaries were over, celebrities were introduced in the ring. While the announcer boomed their names, Dempsey, thinking of the hundreds of hoboes who waited outside, said quietly to the chief usher, "Throw the gates open."

A horde of begrimed men surged into the upper portion of the arena.

During the fight, which was between Max Baer and Paulino Uzcudun, the latter's seconds complained to Dempsey that Baer was butting.

Dempsey looked at the Basque's bleeding forehead. "Butt him back," he snapped, "Butt him back." Baer soon grunted from the impact of a head even harder than his own.

Dempsey circled the bleeding antagonists, saying over and over, "Come on boys, it's a fight."

For business reasons, he wanted Baer to win. A native of the region, he would draw better in a future fight. But the last round over, he declared Uzcudun the winner.

The men of the press attended a dinner that night. Dempsey and a dozen bruisers waited upon the table.

Wilson Mizner presided. The paunch of his two-hundred and seventy pound body resting on the table, he looked at Dempsey and said, "Gentlemen—we are being waited upon by better men than ourselves."

All looked at Dempsey.

"That's according to the way you look at it," he said.

The banquet was attended by a dozen of Uzcudun's countrymen who owned sheep ranches in Nevada. They carried large canvas bags, heavy with wine. In the midst of Mr. Mizner's sentimental peroration, every Basque lifted his bag at arm's length and squirted wine straight into the orator's mouth with the scientific precision of a policeman shooting an innocent bystander.

When the laughter subsided, Dempsey solemnly said, "Boys, you are not showing Mr. Mizner the proper respect. He has a right to talk, and, as this will be our last chance to be together, we ought to listen to him."

Mizner was soon lost again in his maze of far-gone hyperbole:

"Gentlemen, with us will go the days of far-gone glory. We have met here for a fleeting moment to grasp from remorseless time this happy occasion. Though we live in a land where every man is his brother's jailer, we, at least, are a group of thoughtful travellers between the nebulous shores of eternity. For we have learned that—

"Friendship is a golden chain
That binds us all together;
And if that chain we never break,
We shall be friends forever—"

And never before have I seen so fine a gathering."

Suddenly he shouted, "My God, is there something burning?"

He looked at his feet.

Uzcudun had crawled along the floor the whole length of the table and given him a "hotfoot".

Mizner grabbed a scorched foot and roared, "You're a bunch of brigands and cut-throats, with dull razors.

The only reason your mothers didn't drink poison the day you were born, was because there was none in the house."

The dinner served, Dempsey seated himself near me and looked at a picture of Jeffries and Johnson taken in the ring at Reno at the time of their fight for the world's heavyweight championship. Many dignitaries were photographed with the pugilists.

Jeffries, as if balancing the burden of the white race, stood with his knotty legs wide apart. His partly bald head was slightly bowed—the symbol of a man upon whom defeat was written.

Johnson's head was thrown back. On his dark face was a wide smile.

Dempsey stared at the picture.

"I wish I'd have been there in Jeff's place," he said.

I asked, "Did you ever enjoy beating one fighter more than another?"

"No, I guess not," was the answer. "It's a kind of war. You shoot or get shot."

There was a pause.

"Maybe," he went on, "I did get more of a thump than usual out of beating Carl Morris, the original White Hope. I'd been his sparring partner in Kansas City, and when I left him I was flat broke, with nothing but a cheap blue serge suit, a sweater, and a pair of tights in a pasteboard suitcase.

"Before I bummed a ride out of town on a blind baggage, I asked Carl to send the suitcase to me, so I'd have some clean clothes when I landed in Pueblo.

"It was hard riding, but I beat it through in two days. I went after my suitcase and found that Morris hadn't sent it yet. When it came, four days later, the fellow at the express-office told me there was two dollars' charge on it. That was a knockout, for I didn't have a dime. I was all day raising the money—a man I knew at a pool hall finally lent it to me.

"I got some fights through Colorado and Utah, and landed in 'Frisco about a year later. The four-round game was booming, and, it wasn't long till they matched me with Morris.

"He slapped me on the back the day before the fight and said, 'Hello there, Jack! You're comin' up in the world. I hate to make you slip!'

"'You won't make me slip, Pardner,' I said to him. 'Remember the time you shipped my suitcase to me in Pueblo, collect?' Before he could answer, I said, 'So do I —and I'll tell you more about it tomorrow night.' "

"What happened?" I asked.

"Plenty," was the answer, "I knocked him out in a minute—nearly drove my fist through his heart."

This is the only time, to my knowledge, that he ever carried animus into the ring. He speaks kindly of all the men he has ever fought, except Sharkey, the former champion, whom he knocked out in seven rounds, "I can whip him when I'm eighty," he says.

The turbulent tide in Dempsey's life turned in 1917, when Jack Kearns became his manager. At that time, after more than seven years in the ring, he was still not an extraordinary performer.

It was agreed between them that Kearns was to receive fifty percent of all the money that Dempsey earned. No papers were signed.

Jack Kearns had been a one-time mediocre welterweight. He had emerged from his many beatings in the ring with a brain as cunning in its sphere as that of Talleyrand.

A typical Irishman, blase, sentimental, cruel and kind by turns, he knew every dark winding lane in the most crooked business in the world.

With a kind of perception close to genius, he knew, in his tawdry, punch-drunk world, exactly how to get what he wanted from men less astute than himself. Superior to his environment, this one-time bruiser is worthy of more than passing notice in the dingy realms of the manly art.

* * * * * * *

The break came when Dempsey married Estelle Taylor. Kearns opposed the marriage. Poor Dempsey soon had two managers, and a maze of trouble. He found excuses to break his verbal agreement with Kearns. A few months before his first fight with Tunney, he said to me, "You see, I'm married now. A fifty-fifty split with Kearns is too much. I must look after my wife."

She was then earning from twenty-five to fifty thousand dollars a year as a movie actress.

Within the year, Dempsey was matched with Gene Tunney for the championship. Harrassed on all sides by lawyers engaged by Kearns, he was to pay dearly for what some thought was his one mistake. Even the woman was soon to go.

Philadelphia was crowded. Twelve reporters, myself among them, bunked in one hotel room.

Jack McAuliffe, the undefeated lightweight champion of forty years ago, lay on the bed, drinking black coffee heavily blended with whiskey.

A newspaper story was being sent out under his name. It predicted how the fight would end.

McAuliffe, his moon-face wrinkled, paid no attention to the story he was supposed to be writing.

When I poured more liquor in his cup, the cagey old conqueror of young Griffo, the world's greatest boxer, confided, "If you got any money on Dempsey, Jimmy, cover it—he's fightin' things he can't hit today."

"He's lost a great manager," a reporter said.

Another cut in: "For a dame who won't stick."

A man entered the room and handed McAuliffe a ten-dollar bill.

"Is that all you could get for a twenty-seven dollar ticket?" The old fighter crumpled the money and sighed, "Well, it didn't cost me nothin'."

"Aren't you going to the fight, Jack?" Damon Runyon asked.

"No," was the answer. "I've seen a fight."

When a noted Western gambler's name was announced, Damon Runyon said, "If this bird'll tell you how he's betting, you can tell how the fight's going."

Upon entering, he was asked, "How are you betting, Walter?"

"On Tunney," was the answer.

"How much?"

"Fifty thousand."

At five that afternoon we went to the ringside. Loaded with sandwiches, coffee, and a dozen pints of whiskey, we took our seats. Torn clouds drifted above the wide bowl, which, in a few hours, was to be filled with more than a hundred thousand people.

Tex Rickard's army of ushers were called, stood at their posts, courteous to all.

Rain-clouds hung low when the first preliminary started at eight-thirty. It was raining when Tunney and Dempsey entered the ring.

We, who had long known the ways of the ring, looked at Dempsey, then from one to the other.

The first round revealed that the spring was gone

from his powerful body. His judgment of distance, that priceless attribute of the pugilist, was no more.

The rain fell harder. It slanted between the lights above the ring, and squished from the gloves when blows were delivered.

Soon the ring was a pool of water.

Beween the ninth and tenth rounds a dapper man in a checked suit tried to get into the ring and talk to Dempsey.

He was held in his seat.

When the fight was over, the announcer yelled, "Ladies and gentlemen—a new champion!"

The galleries were stunned. Then, slowly, in the pouring rain, loud cheers came from many thousands.

With a towel over his head, water and blood dripping down his lithe body, the mightiest gladiator of all time stumbled from the ring.

The dapper man in the checked suit looked at him with tear-filled eyes.

It was Jack Kearns.

DIEGO RIVERA

DIEGO RIVERA

Diego Rivera met me in Mexico City. He was a large, shy man, with a diffident manner. He had the expression of a man whom a beggar would approach on the street. His eyes were soft, sad and wide apart. Their softness belied the hard brain behind them. More than six feet tall, he was extremely heavy.

He was dressed in a well-made blue suit of excellent material, with an expensive scarf to match.

His weight seemed to bend his knees. And yet, he was agile.

There was something Oriental about him, an impassive quality that was yet full of life and meaning.

Even had I not known who he was, my observation of humans would have told me that I was in the presence of no ordinary man. His hands were well moulded. The fingers tapered. His hair was raven-black and long, his forehead high.

He greeted me politely, and became silent. The man who had defied the Rockefellers was at a loss for words. He scanned me as though I were one of the hated bourgeoisie. We entered a nearby restaurant. His business manager and another gentleman seated themselves at the table with us. The artist toyed with his knife and fork, and after a few preliminaries, asked, "Why do you come so far to see me, and not one of the workers?" He spoke English slowly.

"Well, I'd have a hell of a time getting an editor to

79

allow me to write an article about a Mexican worker. His readers are more apt to be interested in you."

He said nothing in return, but sat quite still, his elbows on the table, his ponderous shoulders sagging. He looked at his knife as though it were a sword.

"But there's millions of workers here," he finally said.

"And one Rivera," I countered.

His eyes shot swiftly at me. He looked downward again at his knife, as I said, "We need you in America, and we want to understand you. I wish you could paint your murals on the clouds." He became slightly warmer, and more relaxed, but made no mention of the compliment.

The usual Communistic generalities followed. Being a polite man, he bored me with no economic facts. He knew Stalin and Trotzky and believed Stalin a less able man than the latter . . . a peasant in his mind. Then his words came more slowly, "No matter what opinion I shall have about the policy of Stalin, my first duty is to all the workers all over the world, and the defense of the Soviet Union."

His business manager explained that Senor Rivera had come from an unpleasant experience that morning. The great artist acquiesced.

I liked him.

It was the first of many meetings I was to have with him.

DIEGO RIVERA

The huge Mexican is best known to millions in America because of his quarrel with the Rockefellers. Having dared to paint a picture of Lenin on one of their walls, they dared to have it removed. There was justice on both sides, but humor was not in between.

It is not likely that Mr. Stalin would have ordered the face of John D. Rockefeller to be painted on the walls of a building in Russia. A study of the colossus-minded Lenin's life reveals a man as fanatical as Luther. But he did have a bitter humor, and he might have used such a picture as an object lesson to the children and have it captioned—TEACH ERRING MAN TO SPURN THE RAGE OF GAIN.

The Rockefellers were at a disadvantage in that certain economic forces were against their point of view. Otherwise, they were within their rights even though it may be questioned whether or not, in destroying the picture they did not make a mistake. Posterity might also doubt the wisdom of their treatment of one considered by many the greatest muralist since Michelangelo. For people who believe that wealth should only be held in trust, though they do not say for how long, they were certainly without far vision.

Rivera had just completed his gigantic conception of Human Intelligence in Control of the Forces of Nature. He considered this to be his masterpiece, and all was apparently going well with the artist in the haunts of the

Rockefellers. Knowing the history of Standard Oil, he had ironically devised such a caption.

Across the top of this mural, the bland and disrespectful Communist had grouped many grim soldiers, wearing gas masks. These patriotic gentlemen were about to launch an attack on columns of Rivera's beloved workers and peasants, who were singing, perhaps, "The Internationale." In the center of this mural he had painted the head of a worker, brooding over a television machine. The model for the worker was the nephew of the deposed leader of Tammany Hall—John F. Curry.

Below this pageant of our history were radicals carrying banners, which read, "FREE TOM MOONEY" and "WE WANT WORK, NOT CHARITY." The police were pictured bouncing clubs off the heads of the radicals. And near all this was a picture of society people playing bridge.

This was disturbing. Rivera was not satisfied. Out of all this emerged a barrel-shaped man with a moon-round face. It was Lenin. He was joining the hands of a white worker and a Negro.

That was too much. Señor Rivera received a letter from John D. Rockefeller's grandson, Nelson Rockefeller, which read:

"I noticed that in the most recent portion of the painting you had included a portrait of Lenin. The piece is beautifully painted, but it seems to me that this portrait, appearing in this mural, might very easily offend a great many people. If it were in a private house it would be one thing, but the mural is in a public building, and the situation is therefore quite different. As much as I dislike to do so, I am afraid we must ask you to substitute the face of some unknown man where Lenin's face now appears."

Rivera promptly answered that to balance Lenin, the unknown man he would substitute would be Abraham Lincoln freeing the slaves, or John Brown.

Mr. Rivera was called to the main office, like any other employee, and fired.

His check for $14,000, the balance of his $21,000 contract, was paid him in full.

The incident shook the economic heavens for a second. Millions of newspaper readers glanced at the headlines, and noticing that the Rockefellers were in trouble again, they turned to the latest murder.

Rivera made a speech shortly afterward in which he explained that it had all been a part of a propaganda mission which he had started on his last visit to America. At that time two people were highly enthusiastic about an exhibition of his work. They were Mrs. John D. Rockefeller, Jr., and her son, Nelson.

Then, Rivera told the assemblage, that friends in Moscow, where he had been some years before, had told him that in all cases the workers and peasants were right, and that the artist should paint what he wanted. He explained that he had then decided to try his propaganda in an industrial country. "In order to get here I had to do as a man in war. Sometimes, in times of war, a man disguises himself as a tree. My paintings in this country have become increasingly and gradually clearer."

So the Rockefellers thought.

If ethically one leans toward the Rockefellers, the greater sympathy should go to the Mexican. A giant should beware of battles with pygmies. There are so many of them.

A short time before, Rivera's more narrow-minded Communists objected to his advertising of Capitalistic enterprise in his work.

If Rivera believes that the purpose of art is to preach the ideas of the individual artist, he has succeeded beyond any man of his time. And yet, when Rockefeller had the Lenin mural destroyed, he called it "cultural vandalism." He preferred, however, to see it destroyed rather than alter it.

A leading American critic of the arts, Thomas Craven, contrasting Diego Rivera with his Mexican contemporary, José Clemente Orozco, says, "Of the two, Rivera, with an ingratiating innocence which conceals his cunning opportunism, is the more prominent."

That Rivera is an ingratiating man, no student of human nature can deny. His cunning opportunism, if he has it, is not for himself. It springs from his pity for those who do the labor of the world and share not its rewards.

Except that he is greater as a man, than was poor one-eared Vincent Van Gogh, their hearts beat in unison with pain. Van Gogh, who died a maniac, wrote to his brother, "When you have attended the free lectures of the College of Misery, you will reap a firm faith, and learn more than you can express in words. Many a man has a bonfire in his heart and nobody comes to warm himself at it. The passers-by notice only a little smoke from the chimney, and go their way. I am drawn more and more to the conclusion that to love much is the best means of approaching God. I am trying to save my soul . . . . Disdaining marble, clay and color, I am working in living flesh and blood, as did Christ, the greatest of all artists."

Rivera might smile at the allusion to Christ. He is not sentimental. Unlike most artists, he has capacity for deep thought, and a sweeping diabolical sense of irony.

The Communistic artist speaks of the worker, the bourgeois, the proletariat, as naively as a Greenwich Village intellectual.

The mastery of irony with the brush is not shocked with Anatole France: that men should be so positive about things, when one has sought so long without finding, and when in the end one remains in doubt. Martyrs are lacking in irony; it is an unpardonable fault, for without irony the world would be like a forest without birds;

irony is the gaiety of meditation and the joy of wisdom. What further? I charge the martyrs with fanaticism; I suspect a kind of natural kinship between them and their executioners, and I fancy that, were they the stronger, they would take the place of the executioners. Doubtless I am wrong. Still, I am supported by history. It shows me Calvin between the faggots prepared for him, and those that he kindles; it shows me Henry Estienne, who was at great pains to escape the executioners of the Sorbonne, denouncing Rabelais as deserving the whole range of torments . . . . .

The wise Frenchman would have found an ironical problem in Rivera, who might still be incited to borrow the oil from John D. Rockefeller and prepare the faggots for one with whom he violently disagreed.

He was never strictly a worker, no more so than was Lenin. They saw human misery as children and decided to remember it.

To those who believe that the meanest beggar will eventually have his pockets full of stars, there are tremendous possibilities in the fact that a man of Rivera's great ability can remain so deeply imbedded in the earth, and can still be so completely fundamental that he can cry with a hurt child, or rise in rebellion with a lash-scarred slave.

He carries a heavy revolver strapped to his side. The large man, with the wide moon face, and the soft calf eyes, with a revolver strapped to his side, is one of the incongruities of nature. The big fellow has need of his gun. The Nazis recently put two bullets through the upper windows of his home. He points to them and smiles, with his ingratiating innocence.

He was born in 1886, the place Guanajuato, Mexico, where his father was a chemical engineer in a silver mine. He blends Spanish, Russian, Indian, and Jewish blood. His maternal great-grandfather was a Tarascan Indian. His father's mother was a Portugese Jewess. Rivera's mother was born in Mexico, of Spanish decent.

He attaches no importance to his being a Mexican more by environment than blood. He shrugged his immense shoulders when I tried to trace the influence of his ancestors. "The books of Karl Marx, and life itself, are my greatest influences—all countries my blood, all people my pity. I have no national feelings."

"How have you accomplished so much work?"

"Because I am a worker, and not an artist. I work like every other man. I do not have the temperament of the artist. I am not pretentious." The last word bothered him but he managed it.

"Are you and Orozco friends?"

"I have no friends, and no enemies. I only care for what is useful for the workers."

"But surely you have much in common with Orozco—you must like him."

His big head shook. "I like his painting—I do not like him, and—he does not like me . . . . I have taken his part here against the bureaucrats."

"Then why does he not like you?"

"Because I was once asked to finish his work. No artist ever forgave another for that," he answered.

Rivera has always been in sympathy with the aims of Zapata. To many he was a common murderer. To Rivera, he remains an idealistic Indian who wanted to restore the land to his people.

About twenty years ago, three per cent of the population owned 97% of all land, houses, and other sources of production in Mexico. One huge hacienda consisted of one-fiftieth of the land of Mexico, an area about as large as Holland.

Obregon, Zapata, and especially the strong Calles, however mixed their motives might have been, tried to attain more freedom for the vast 97% who owned nothing.

Calles removed the mystical prop upon which millions of Mexicans leaned by closing the churches. He then tried to restore to the great masses of the people liberty, land, and public education. Mexico is no longer a paradise for the foreign exploiter of other human beings, as it was in the days of Diaz. But it has no depression.

All this is of importance here. For out of the chaos of its preceding revolutions have emerged two of the greatest artists in the world—Rivera and Orozco.

Rivera knows men.

"What about Madero?" I asked him.

"He was very good and very weak—the United States helped him against Zapata—the bourgeoisie against the peasant."

"And Villa?"

"Extremely intelligent, the typical bourgeois revolutionist, the small rancher who wanted to be a landlord, the instrument of the English and the Germans, and the tool of the Mexican Catholic Church—Zapata was different—when Madero offered him much land, he said, "I don't want land for myself, but for all the peasants of Mexico.""

He has deep hatred for those who exploit peasants. In one of his pictures, a group of them labor in a field. It is so vivid, they seem to move. A master stands over them with a long whip. As we looked at it together, a smile spread across Rivera's face. He pointed to the master, and said, "They liquidated him soon after." It was his way of describing assassination.

Rivera's harshest American critic, Thomas Craven, quarrels with his American murals, saying they are crowded with wooden Indians, stock figures and the insignia of Communism. The same critic, whose otherwise keen penetration becomes slightly blurred when he thinks of the Mexican artist, has written, "If there is anything in art that may be set down as a certainty, it is the fact that participation of some sort is indispensable to appreciation.

A DOZEN AND ONE

To know and understand a work of art, one must be able to enter into it, to participate in the spirit that created it. One cannot remain apart, especially above it, and appreciate its values or measure its appeal.

As one who has known the road, the ring, the factory, and the jail, I admire Rivera's American scenes. Mooney and Haywood in prison, Sacco and Vanzetti waiting for the life-destroying juice, the whipped people crying for bread under the lash of the economic masters, all speak to me as fluently as Walt Whitman. If my testimony is worthless, we will call Einstein to the stand, who says to Rivera of the same murals, "I take advantage of this opportunity to express to you my great admiration. No other artist of our days could have impressed me in this manner. I wish that the whole world could recognize more and more what an asset you are to it."

Seeing Thomas Craven's "Men of Art" on his shelf, I pointed to it. He shook his head quickly and said emphatically, "No, no."

"But he called you a learned Mexican," I ventured.

He thought for a moment and returned, "That's because I can still teach him much about art."

Many of Rivera's murals are too crowded. It is as if the great artist feared that he would run out of walls upon which to paint his fancies. When I explained this to him, my reward was a benignant smile.

Neither did I consider his portraits of living people

quite so successful. "It's too bad that a man of your scope must do such things," I said.

"I don't get many to do," he returned tiredly, "I flatter them not enough," said the genius for caricature.

"What would you do if you made a million at such work?"

"Give it all to the workers," replied the man of simple faith, in and out of whose home Mexican laborers go with their talks of strikes, lockouts, and boycotts.

Never have I seen men of any rank receive more intense attention and consideration than is given them by the ponderous Communist. His social creed may be right or wrong, according to the viewpoint. No man can doubt his compassion for his less gifted kind.

A man of taste, he appreciates good living.

"I was amazed," said an American writer to me, "at his knowledge of rare wines and excellent food."

But now he is strict with his diet. Having once weighed more than three hundred pounds, he has reduced a hundred.

And all about him is the harmony of color. Fifteen years in Europe, and extensive travel, combined with extraordinary mental capacity, have made him a genuine cosmopolitan. In moods, he becomes loquacious. At other times he is solemn, his sad eyes full of wonder.

His home, in a suburb of Mexico City, is surrounded with a spiraled cactus fence. The gate has a lock upon it, though one can spread the cactus apart and step into the yard.

His home is in two units. They are three and four stories high and of modern construction. One building is the color of red earth, the other is cobalt blue.

As Mrs. Rivera is also an artist, they have separate studios. Their working needs are in one building, their domestic interests in another. The buildings are connected by a bridge which runs from the top floor terrace to the sun roof of the other. Rivera's studio is two stories high, and one side is entirely of glass. Hundreds of pieces of Mexican sculpture are on wooden shelves. Immense dummies hang on the walls. At one end is a large picture of a field of cactus, painted by Rivera. Each cactus, twisted in the shape of an imploring hand, reaches upward.

"I like the cactus," said Rivera. "It is like people— only different—so strong."

His affection for his wife was charming. He called her *chiquita*—little girl. She graces some of his murals. She also had a record in the rebellion. Unassuming, and not talkative, she was natural as dawn. Her own paintings adorn her studio. A few reveal talent. One is of a child being born.

While accompanying Rivera and a portly American woman, of the inhibited period, through the studio, the artist, either naively, or with malicious intent, handed her this painting. She glanced at the realistic scene of the woman in birth agony, and blushed, speechless. Her hands trembled, while the painter watched, with ingratiating innocence.

Finally she said feebly, "That's very ni---I mean," and handed it to Rivera. He returned it to its place with the dignity of a Chinese mandarin.

Rivera is never so much at home as when painting Indians. These people, with their centuries old incrustation of mystified stolidity, awaken his wonder. In the Ministry of Education he has placed two Indians in one of his best murals. The somnolent figures merely embrace each other. All the tragedy of life is in the embrace.

His small library contains such diverse books as my friend, Jim Steven's PAUL BUNYAN, GULLIVER'S TRAVELS, Faure's HISTORY OF ART, and my own SHADOWS OF MEN.

"I like Stevens, and the life he describes." Then he explained, "I do not read much now. I have not the time."

He has read two other Americans, on account of their Communistic leanings, John Dos Passos, and Mike Gold.

"Good men," he said. I agreed.

"Some day I shall illustrate one of your books."

I thanked him.

When I mentioned the name of Ambassador Josephus Daniels, Rivera said, "He ordered the bombardment of Vera Cruz."

"It was his job as Secretary of the Navy at the time," I said.

"Yes, I know." He paused and I continued, "And he told me yesterday that he did not care whether a man was a Methodist, a Catholic, or a Communist, so long as he was a fine artist."

The remark pleased him. He smiled ."I have heard that your President Roosevelt is of the same opinion."

Daniels is now popular with the Mexican people. His remark, "I have been a life-long resident of Mexico for two years," is often quoted by them.

Rivera places Walter Pach and Ernestine Evans first among the artists and critics in America who encouraged and appreciated him. Frederick Leighton and Lee Simonson follow. John Sloan and Alfred Stieglitz were also early supporters.

William Spratling, an American writer living in Mexico, told me how one man discovered Rivera.

He was bored with Mexico and threatened to leave.

"Why not come with me to meet Diego Rivera?" Spratling suggested.

"Who is Diego Rivera?" asked the man.

After he had been informed, he went with Spratling to see Rivera, who was then widely known. Later the man told the New York public of the great Mexican artist he had discovered.

Many there are who feel that the Communist is throttling the artist in Rivera. It may place him under a temporary cloud in capitalistic countries, but it can never smother the burning genius of the man so long as there are walls upon which he can paint.

Happy when painting murals, he still looks forward to a future in the United States. The vast forces of this nation, its mills and mines and factories strongly appeal to him. Along with his famous contemporary, Orozco, he has exalted his own nation. He may yet exalt ours.

There are tolerant men and women in America. I can hear the roars of the Communists. The Rockefellers tried, within their limitations, to meet Rivera half way. He might have compromised a trifle. He could have got away with everything else. Suppose he had given Lenin a beard and called him Moses. The art critics would have known the difference, and all would have been serene.

Then Lenin could have cried under his disguise, while the great social forces of mankind remained embroiled as of old, with lust and greed, passion and pity, and the thousand and one knaveries, deceits and sentimentalities, which no legislation will ever eradicate on this insignificant bubble in the vast cauldron of the Universe.

GEORGE JEAN NATHAN

GEORGE JEAN NATHAN

He has the manner of a man too bored to flick the ashes from a cigarette. Above middle height, he is dark, with brown eyes. Well tailored, immaculate, he is fully conscious that he is George Jean Nathan. His voice is deep and pleasing. Though forced to study piano for eight of his formative years, he still loves good music.

He wears his opinions with nonchalance, and talks neither loud nor long. No man I have ever known has a greater power of attention. It is respectful, intense.

Born with money, he has not been twisted by violent economic storms. He can make allowances, however, for the gales through which his friends have passed.

As a critic, even of that which a friend has written, he is impersonal as the weather.

He has lived for twenty-five years in a small apartment on a busy New York street. It is within walking distance of the theatre, which makes up half his life. Sombre, it fits his brooding temperament. In one room is a large desk. Strewn upon it are many pencils and fountain pens. He writes slowly, laboriously, in long hand. Words his painful medium, his finished work has often the effect of being welded at white heat. Unusual among critics, he can create a mood.

Called a snob by many, his aloofness is a wall built to fortify himself against boredom. Not a lover of people in the mass, he has a horror of those who pretend. This keeps his circle small. Those in the enclosure remain for years.

He speaks of Theodore Dreiser, Eugene O'Neil, Sinclair Lewis and H. L. Mencken with affection. They have "size". It is a word he uses for those who have deep compassion and understanding.

The greatest dramatic critic in the world, he has none of the mob's diversions. He does not believe in exercise after one is forty. "If you walk you get cinders in your eyes."

When pretty young women talk of art, literature, philosophy or the drama, he listens politely, the cigarette upward, with an inch of ash. Overjoyed they watch the interest in his eyes. He hears not a word they say. It is vibrancy, beauty, the rare sheen on the growing flower that attracts him.

If with de Maupassant he might ask—what can women say to God?—he is aware of their charm and beauty.

His idea of a perfect wife is Mrs. Eugene O'Neil. For Sara Haardt, the charming and talented girl who married H. L. Mencken, he had affection and admiration.

Intelligently sad, a lover of laughter, the sparkle of rare wine, the curves of a youthful lady, it is often dark weather in the heart of Nathan. As the years verge beyond fifty, his melancholy deepens. When Percy Hammond, his friend and fellow critic, died, he said to me, "One by one the old parade is passing."

He was born in Fort Wayne, Indiana. His father was Charles Naret Nathan, the owner of vineyards in France and coffee plantations in Brazil. Speaking eight languages, he was a world rover, having spent a great deal of time in China, India, France, America and the Argentine.

His grandfather was a well-known Parisian lawyer. An uncle was a professor in the University of Brussels. His mother, Ella Nirdlinger, was born in Fort Wayne, and educated at a Notre Dame convent.

The greater part of his boyhood was spent in Cleveland, Ohio.

His uncle, Charles Frederic Nirdlinger, a dramatic critic and the author of now forgotten plays, the translator of Echegaray's drama made popular in America by William Faversham under the title of "The World and His Wife", was a deciding influence in his career.

At fifteen, he studied Elizabethan and Greek drama under his uncle's tutelage. He was in Europe three times as a student before entering Cornell.

When it was planned to send him to Harvard, as a mater of family pride, his uncle having graduated there, Nathan decided on Cornell. "I never could bring myself to view Harvard as the right place for me," he said. "I did not like what it stood for—its English imitativeness was offensive to me. I chose Cornell for the simple reason that it seemed to me of all the Eastern American universities to approach the German university most closely. I still believe that it does. Various eminent German scholars, incidentally, agree in this. In addition, it is a charming and beautiful place."

Specializing for four years in literature, drama, language and psychology, he obtained a Bachelor's degree. His interests were many in college. Editor of The Cornell Widow, he was a member of the Kappa Sigma Fraternity, Senior Honorary Society, the Quill and Dagger, the Savage Club, the Sunday Night Club and the Masque. He was even chairman of Cornell Spring Day, the annual circus and jamboree of the institution.

He was not impressed by professors. "Some boys go to college and eventually succeed in getting out. Others go to college and never succeed in getting out. The latter are called professors."

He further asked, "Is there a college or university in America whose professors of English composition would have given a mark higher than minus one to George Ade, Helen Green, Ring Lardner, Kin Hubbard, Edgar Lee Masters and Walter Hasenclever, had they come before them as young, unknown men and women?"

He graduated from Cornell at twenty-two. A year later he was given a diploma by the University of Bologna in Italy.

His uncle then secured him a position on the New

GEORGE JEAN NATHAN

York Herald at fifteen dollars a week.

Within a year he wrote a three column story of a race he did not see. It was listed on the bulletin board of the editorial room as an object in vivid writing.

Promoted to the Sunday department, his work consisted in writing two feature stories a week. They averaged three and four thousand words in length. His weekly salary was thirty dollars. He soon began to write dramatic criticism. The first play he reviewed was by Lincoln J. Carter.

When the city editor asked him to cover police stations, Nathan refused on the ground that his talents had grown beyond such work. He was told that it would be a great experience. Nathan considered the editor's viewpoint as "one of the schnitzels of buncombe with which newspaper men delude themselves."

After resigning from the Herald he met Lynn G. Wright. Like Nathan he had been an editor at Cornell. Wright employed Nathan as dramatic critic on two magazines he was editing.

He next joined H. L. Mencken as editor of the "Smart Set". It soon became one of the most brilliant magazines ever published in America.

Lampooning the old standards of expression, they became famous. Editorials were written about them.

A well known jingle by Berton Braley went across the nation:

A DOZEN AND ONE

There were three that sailed away one night
Far from the maddening throng,
And two of the three were always right
And everyone else was wrong.

But they took another along, these two,
To bear them company,
For He was the only One ever knew
Why the other two should be.
And so they sailed away, these three—
  Mencken,
  Nathan,
  And God.

And the two they talked of the aims of art,
Which they alone understood,
And they quite agreed from the very start
That nothing was any good,
Except some novels that Dreiser wrote
And some plays from Germany.
When God objected, they rocked the boat
And dropped Him into the sea,
"For You have no critical facultee,"
  Said Mencken
  And Nathan
  To God.

The two came cheerfully sailing home
Over the surging tide,
And trod once more on their native loam,
Wholly self-satisfied.

And the little group that calls them great
Welcome them fawningly.
Though why the rest of us tolerate
This precious pair must be
Something nobody else can see
> But Mencken
> Nathan
> And God!

Giving up the "Smart Set," they became editors of "The American Mercury." Confining himself more and more to the theatre, Nathan soon withdrew from the task, and became contributing dramatic editor.

Much has been said about the rift between them. It was never serious.

Better than all others, Nathan has pegged Mencken: "He is my friend. He favors bloody wars in which hundreds of thousands meet their death, and collects cigar bands for his little four year old niece. He is a champion of the Nietzschean doctrine, and spend considerable time each year in toy stores picking out doll babies and choo-choo cars for the youngsters of his married acquaintances. He has above the writing table a large framed photograph of the Iron Chancellor, and on his writing table a small framed photograph of a very prety girl. He chews tobacco and his favorite musical compositions are the waltzes of Johann Strauss.

"He is a foe of democracy and politely sees every

person, however asinine, who comes to call on him. He believes and stoutly maintains that one strong enemy is more valuable than two mediocre friends, and then makes friends with the strong enemy soon after he shows up. He is in favor of a merciless autocracy and collects postage stamps for his brother's little child. He is a rabid anti-prohibitionist and gets a violent attack of heartburn and a sour middle whenever he drinks two cocktails.

"He scorns society, but has his evening clothes made by one of the best and most expensive of Fifth Avenue tailors. He lustily derides golf players and amuses himself every afternoon playing with some pet turtles in his back yard. He writes vehemently against quack doctors and has tried ten of them in an anempt to get rid of his hay fever. He insists that he likes only the company of middle-aged women, and associates solely with young ones. He ridicules any man who is vain in the matter of personal appearance, and goes out and buys a new necktie if the one he has with him does not match the shirt he is wearing. He is an exponent of the "Be hard" doctrine, is in favor of killing off the weak, and sends milk twice a month to the starving babies of the war-ridden European countries. He is a fatalist and doses himself daily with a half dozen various philtres."

And Mencken says: "We differ in many ways. Nathan is greatly amused at the theatre even when it is bad, whereas I regard it as a bore even when it is good. Contrariwise, I am much interested in politics, whereas Nathan scarcely knows who is vice-president of the United States."

As an editor with Mencken he encouraged such writers as Sherwood Anderson, Ben Hecht, Eugene O'Neill, James Huneker, George Ade, James Branch Cabell, Carl Sandburg and Willa Cather.

With Mencken he was the first to give an American audience to Havelock Ellis, Lord Dunsany, Ibsen, Hauptmann, Strindberg, Sudermann, Nietzsche and Shaw.

When Ray Long of Cosmopolitan refused W. Somerset Maugham's "Miss Thompson," it was published in "Smart Set." Among Maugham's great stories, it was dramatized as "Rain" and became the talk of the nation.

Many of his reflections are not unworthy of La Rochefoucauld.

"The most pitiable of all human emotions is the gayety of despair."

"It is only strong men who suffer pain from petty tragedies."

"The most beautiful and attractive of women loses much of her beauty and attractiveness when she becomes emphatic."

"Great drama is the reflection of a doubt in the heart of a great sad gray man."

A bachelor, he can enjoy long solitude and revel in the gloomy day.

"The beautiful day, the day of blue and gold and sunshine, is God's gift to the plain people; the bad day, the day of gloom and gray and rain, he has reserved for the exclusive pleasure of the aristocracy. The artist, the connoisseur of emotions, the philosopher, these have no use for the fair day; it distracts them, summons them from their introspection and solitude, calls them into the open. On such a day work and those pleasures dear to men with a taste for the sequestered are impossible; the outside beckons too persuasively and too disconcertedly. But when the world is full of wet and fog and the monotony of rain, then the artist, the connoisseur of quiet ,the philosopher and all their brothers are happy. For it is on such days when the yokelry is melancholy because it cannot be eating dill pickles and cheese sandwiches on the roadsides, or riding in Fords through the Jersey swamps, or chasing little white gutta-percha balls across the grass with a repertoire of clubs, that men of soul and sadness revel in the happiness that only God's elect can comprehend."

In arranging a meeting between himself and Jack Dempsey, I said, "You'll find him the best dressed man in New York." Nathan, who might claim such an honor, was instantly alert. The great bruiser, wearing his expensive clothes as easily as a tiger does its skin, using words as forceful as the blows that slaughtered Firpo, was not embarrassed. The texture and coloring of the pugilist's attire did not escape Nathan. When Dempsey left the table for a moment, he said, "You're right."

Jack later gave a "literary dinner" in my honor. Lest I be lost at such an affair, Nathan cancelled a previous engagement to accompany me. We watched the men of words arrive.

Edgar Lee Masters, slightly bent, tired and lonely looking, was brought to our table.

Soon a loud voice asked, "Is Jimmy Tooley here?" Like the Biblical pictures of Moses, the speaker's beard was long and red. Six feet six, he was very broad. His cap, with a pasteboard beak, and several sizes too small, was perched on the top of his large head. He had a wooden leg. Out of his fiery shrubbery peered sincere eyes.

"I'm Peter Freuchen," he said, holding out a ham-like hand.

Breezy as a wind-blown robin, Walter Winchell came next. Others trailed in. The dinner began.

Nathan might have been a professional interviewer, so deeply did he probe Freuchen. That gigantic writer, the greatest ever to invade the North Country, enthralled him. He had married an Eskimo girl. His leg frozen, he had amputated it himself.

"He has genius twice," said Nathan when the huge Dane left. "For writing and living."

"He's quite a man," said Dempsey.

Edgar Lee Masters nodded agreement.

Winchell, for once, was silent. His eyes followed Freuchen.

I pondered for a moment the daredevil drama of my colorful land.

Of those at table, two had been road-kids, another a hoofer, one an Illinois bumpkin, another an aristocrat, and the remaining three bubbles of talent who had survived strong winds.

Nathan, who covered his retreat from life with the shrapnel of cynicism had written: "What interests me is life—its music and color, its charm and ease, its humor and its loveliness. The great problems of the world— social, political economic and theological—do not concern me in the slightest. I care not who writes the laws of a country so long as I may listen to its songs. I can live every bit as happily under a king, or even a kaiser, as under a president. One church is as good as another to me; I never enter one anyway, save only to delight in some particularly beautiful stained glass window, or in some fine specimen of architecture, or in the whiskers of the 'Twelve Apostles.'

"What concerns me alone is myself, and the interests of a few close friends. For all I care, the rest of the world may go to hell at today's sunset. I was born in America, and America is to me at the time of writing, the most comfortable country to live in—and also at the time of writing the very pleasantest—in the world.

GEORGE JEAN NATHAN

"Give me a quiet room, a pad of paper, eight or nine sharp lead pencils, a handful of thin, mild cigars, and enough to eat and drink—all of which, by the grace of God, are happily within my means—and I do not care a tinker's damn whether the nations of the earth arm, disarm, or conclude to fight their wars by limiting their armies to biting each other."

Reading this, a caustic critic said that Nathan lacked the imagination to embrace humanity. Rather, he might be called the First Apostle of the Self-Centered with the courage to admit it.

WILSON MIZNER

WILSON MIZNER

He had a long, heavily lined, and powerful horse face. In repose it was careworn—a Holbein done in sadness. Humor was nowhere upon it, not even at the edges of his tired, rheumy eyes, beneath which were sacs of blue. There was a lack of determination about his mouth. It was always slightly open.

Affable and adroit, his smile was never from the heart. With tremendous apprehension and sensibility, he was in reality a vast and grandiloquent pimp to whom all life was a house of prostitution.

Wilson Mizner was born in Northern California, and attended Santa Clara College for two years. After being dismissed, he joined a medicine faker, and early learned the easy exaggeration that characterized him through life.

He reached Alaska in the Gold Rush of 1897. One of the first Americans on the Klondike, he remained five years. Gambler and entertainer, he was one of a group later to be nationally known, among them Tex Rickard, Jack London, Rex Beach, Alexander Pantages, Senator Key Pittman, Robert W. Service and Sid Grauman.

Called the wittiest man in America, he appeared in Who's Who as a dramatist.

He was proud of his ancestry, being able to trace it seventy years. President Harrison had appointed his father a minister to a country in Central America. Mizner would shout with pride that he came of "an old California family." He was a quarter English, the rest Irish. He seldom mentioned his Irish blood. Only when maudlin would he talk of the woman from whom he had inherited wit, charm and a grandiose manner.

He had those qualities so deeply impregnated in the Irish— a revolving heart that could turn hatred into sardonic humor, quick intelligence, extreme volatility, impatience of order, and boundless vanity. There was a salamander in his heart. In heat, it was calm.

His forehead was high, wide and furrowed. His head was large, his hair brown and slightly thinner as he went down the hill of fifty. Six feet, four; a quick moving two hundred and seventy pound man, his hands and feet were too small for his body. He had, in repose, the appearance of an immense leprechaun lost in a world in which he must laugh to keep from crying.

His emotions were permeated with guile. He could dissemble his feelings in an instant. His passions were strong, and even in premature senility were never surpressed.

His shoulders were so straight they seemed to be in a leather brace. To hold in his huge stomach, he walked erect as Ludendorff, with his immense head thrown backward until the neck muscles bulged.

His period, the most colorful in America, had disappeared. Its glittering dust still burned in his eyes. He snorted in never-ending mental agony at the little people around him. As a compensation, they afforded him an audience. Men and women laughed at many of his jokes, the sources of which were dated before Rabelais. The heavy flying fish of wit, he skimmed the surface of all things, and dazzled for a moment in the sun.

An arch flatterer, he had keen penetration.

His compliments fell on all alike.

He dreaded the passing of time. "Only fools have watches—don't time go fast enough?"

On the verge of hypochondria, he would beam with laughter and salutation if approached in public. His giant torso would shake in merriment at a quickly made joke. When the person had gone, he might ask, "Who the hell was that?" He admired crimes of wit, and was horrified at those of violence. He believed in capital punishment for strangers. If the murderer were his friend, he would have freed him at once, with kindly advice.

All people were "outsiders" to him who leaned too heavily on the shoulders of justice. That world of which he so long was a part, knew him as "a dead right guy." A priest might more quickly have betrayed the secrets of a confessional than the garrulous fellow the confidence of a citizen of his world who trusted him. "I have shielded men when I knew they deserved the chair. I couldn't break their confidence and blow a police whistle."

He was cautious in the presence of outsiders. He made famous the saying—never give a sucker an even break. He never did.

A DOZEN AND ONE

At one time in New York he had his fellow confidence men wear roses in their coat lapels as a means of identification. During a hard winter they had begun to prey upon each other.

Gregarious, he could long endure solitude.

He often remained in bed all day and boasted that he had never seen the sun rise.

He appeared wise in all matters he did not comprehend, and covered his ignorance so well that he often deceived the most sagacious. Complex and proud, he seemed simple and unaffected. A scoffer at everything, he secretly worshipped the middle-class proprieties. His manners were suave, and made him appear benevolent toward those whom he scorned.

So long as people were gay, he cared not how shallow they were. This quality made him a favorite in Hollywood.

A well known citizen of the tinsel town, he did not enjoy his popularity.

With hands folded, he would stare at the ceiling.

He lived in one room for six years and always regretted it.

"Why don't you move?" I asked.

"I can never find my other shoe," was the answer.

He liked hotels, and once owned one in New York. A sign read, "Do not smoke opium in the elevator."

A sentimental iconoclast, he fought everything of a

118

subjective nature within himself. He had the capacity without the inclination to think deeply. More than a mere wit, he was the embryo of a great man.

His colossal ego blended with humility.

A bawdy house dialectician, he would rout a more learned man with his wit.

As he seldom associated with superiors, his reputation for wisdom grew.

He retained and used all things that filled his purpose. When he read, "Fame is merely the prolonging of neighborhood gossip," he quoted it often without credit to me.

When I mentioned Schopenhauer's observation, "Dull people are always formal," he exclaimed "Good!" and purloined it.

When told to leave a house he said to his host, "A gentleman never leaves a house until told to do so by a gentleman."

He drove a large, expensive car, the wheel of which no one else ever touched.

He wore a heavy gray overcoat. Pockets bulging with liquor, he would arrive at my home at any hour between dusk and sunrise.

He came one night, forlorn as Lucifer. Three other men accompanied him.

"I'm dyin', Jim," he shouted. "Gimme a drink." He threw his arms upward in despair, and cursed Hollywood. When the liquor touched his brain, his hands gripped the arms of the chair as if he were to be electrocuted.

"You're not talkin' to a local boy, Jimmy." He gulped more liquor.

Suddenly he pulled a sheaf of paper from his pocket.

"You say I'm too lazy to write—listen to this."

While the rain slashed at the windows, he read a story aloud. When he had finished, I said, "That's a great yarn, Bill. I'll wire Joe Medill Patterson of Liberty about it."

The story followed the telegram, and Patterson wired, offering a thousand dollars for it. I telephoned the news to Bill and he complained bitterly, "Lord, it took me eight hours to write that."

As writing was physical labor, he "talked" his stories to a stenographer. When questioned about his method, he said, "All I know about writing is that a cemetery's a period."

As a dramatist, he had been accused of plagiarizing everything with which his name was connected. When I asked him concerning the charges he said, "Didn't Shakespeare steal, you illiterate peasant—and Moliere—and Dante—it's all a stream running nowhere—you dip out the water you need."

"Is it true that one producer died broke, defending lawsuits against you and Paul Armstrong?"

"I came here to drink liquor, not to be questioned, you ditch-digger's cast-off."

Soon he thundered with indignation, "Thirty years

ago I wrote a little song of a hundred and twenty-seven verses. I called it 'Frankie and Johnnie.' Everybody claims that gospel hymn—does it matter?"

"Not at all."

His mouth opened as if jerked with wire. It closed as quickly.

O. Henry had been his friend and favorite writer. "There'll be a bronze statue to O. Henry in every park in the United States a hundred years from now."

In badinage I claimed that I was a better writer than O. Henry. He looked with startled eyes, and snorted, "You—Oh God in Heaven, guide me! What do I hear? You digger in the garbage of literature."

"As you will, Wilson, I'm built to go to far places."

"On a freight." His paunch heaved. "Why you never took a bath till you were thirty years old."

"That may be—but anyone'll tell you that I can write O. Henry's ears off."

His wrath mounted—"Why you impudent, red-headed cur! You porter in the bawdy house of words! My God!" He rose "I'm leaving here right now." He walked a few feet, then turned in further denunciation. "You low rat, you defouler of the great dead, you slime of the underworld, you evasive, shady reprehensible rogue." He paused for breath. "Now I know there's no God, or you'd be struck dead." He looked at me in pitiful scorn. "You, a better writer than O. Henry! Why you couldn't sign his tax receipts! You're as illiterate as a publisher! If you had a Roman nose, you'd be a cinema courtesan." He began to blubber, then shook his head violently. His lips trembled. He took another step. "I'm leaving your house right now, you damned, brainless jazzer of decent English, before you claim you wrote O. Henry's stories."

I said very slowly, "No, Wilson, I wouldn't claim that."

His jowls distended in relief.

"Well," he sighed, "That's one decent thing in you."

"Not exactly decent," was my reply, "I'd be ashamed to."

He fell on the rug and crawled toward the door. "Good God in Heaven!" he screamed, "deliver me from this lousy literary hobo. I'm going!"

He was soon cajoled into having another drink. His arms were around me. His laugh was louder than before. "Only suckers get mad in their liquor."

The telephone rang. My secretary returned with the announcement that Calvin Coolidge was dead.

"How can they tell?" Mizner asked, without looking up.

Grant Clark, the song writer, arrived with a Catholic priest of whom we were both fond.

"Hello, Father," was the play-boy's greeting. "I went

to confession yesterday, and the priest left in the middle of it."

"Where did he go?" asked the priest in surprise.

"For the police," was the answer.

The talk went from life to death. "When you die," Mizner said to his slender friend, "we'll bury you in a fountain pen." Clark was dead in a week. The play-boy was dazed. "The Big Boy up there'll be calling my number next," he said.

He had learned brevity in barrooms and made his points quickly, never talking long. He created thousands of stories. A favorite was: Tim McGrath, an Irish saloon keeper in San Francisco, did not like Negroes. His bartenders were instructed to serve none. One day the Kentucky Rosebud, a mighty colored bruiser, sauntered jauntily into the saloon, and shouted, "Gimme a drink, Bartender."

The server of the drinks snapped, "Give you one—you can't even buy one for a hundred dollars."

The Kentucky Rosebud clutched the bar with his ham-like hands. "If you doan gimme a drink, Ah'll shake youh damn bah down."

The bartender again refused.

He began to shake the bar.

Just then the earthquake came.

When they pulled the bartender and the Kentucky Rosebud out of the debris, the latter pleaded, "Gawd

Almighty—Mistah Bartender—doan' tell Tim I done this."

He had his serious moments.

In Reno we heard of a man executed by gas. When the warden wanted him to make a last request he complied by asking for a gas mask.

With a worried expression, the playboy exclaimed, "And they killed a man with a sense of humor like that."

He delighted in shocking the prudish. His brother was a minister of the Gospel in St. Louis. A leading lady member of his congregation called on Wilson. The talk drifted to early environment.

"My boyhood was full of sin," he confided. "When I first opened my eyes in this world, I found myself in bed with a woman."

After viewing an unusually bad cinema, he said, "Don't miss it if you can."

He had a horror of war, and could not discuss it without a shudder.

His head went from side to side, in wonder at the "unknown soldier's" identity. "A burglar or a saint, it's no matter now."

His favorite verse concerned those fallen in battle:

"They shall not grow old as we that are left
grow old!

Age shall not weary them, nor the years
      condemn.
At the going down of the sun and in the
      morning
We shall remember them."

He would turn the leaves of a book until he found the most daramtic incident. That, he would read and remember.

A paragraph from Huxley, Darwin or Spencer would give the impression that he knew them.

Many books came to him. He would glance through all and place them in a corner of the room.

In time they disappeared.

When away from the crowd, the corners of his large mouth would droop. A haze would creep into his eyes.

The adventurer who had gone down the gay road with laughter was seeing at last the long shadows thrown by the evening sun. "Futility" was a word he often used. It haunted the seemingly happy moments of his life. Knowing that strong liquor would agitate his already enlarged heart, he would gulp huge glasses.

Something had happened to him in Alaska, upon which, except for a few tense moments when the wild horses of delirium dashed through his brain, he was forever silent.

He hated failure, and gravitated toward success as

a moth toward light. A friend might need a thousand dollars; never fifty cents.

To those in his circle he was often warm, considerate, even gentle.

For Jack London, another Alaskan wanderer, he was torn between contempt and envy. He had dared to eclipse the gigantic playboy's fame.

Great as a personality, London was to the playboy merely a "damned romantic liar." Too obtuse to have sympathy for the finest brain and the richest spirit ever to invade the north country, he saw only the obvious in the brililant London. A supreme pantheist, who would endure every insult rather than leave the house of life, the gifted London's reported suicide made him shudder. "There's no hereafter, or Jack would have written a story about it, long and long ago."

For Sid Grauman he retained a lasting affection.

Of Senator Pittman, he spoke with humorous kindness.

Tex Rickard remained for him a "Texas yokel with a lucky break."

"But he had nerve," I once said.

"Burglars have that," was the quick retort.

Toward Alexander Pantages he was vehement to the end.

A physical coward, Mizner was left for dead on a New York street, his jaw broken in many places. Only once did he intimate who might have done it.

Men without humor nursed long hatreds against him. Among them was George Bronson-Howard, whose story, "The Parasite," a vivid picture of shallow lives, defeated its purpose through invective against the pompous playboy.

He smiled in memory of Howard. His hatred was never as deep as his contempt.

"Be urbane to everybody," was his rule. "You can never tell in which pool the next sucker will bite."

A card shark of genius, he would often start "a friendly little game of poker," with Hollywood outsiders. He never lost.

He knew the rudiments of great music. In cadence, he was supreme. Learning to play the piano in boyhood, he developed it further in an Alaskan honky-tonk. To forget the days when gusto had a place in life, the master of pathos and sentimentality would play for hours, and sing to his own accompaniment. His small hands would skim the keys, as he began dolorously:

"Some of them write to the old folks for coin,
That's their ace in the hole.
Others have girls on the old Tenderloin—
That's their ace in the hole.
They'll tell you of all the trips they'll take
From Florida to the North Pole—

But you'll find them next time,
Without clothes or a dime,
If they lost that ace in the hole."

A haunting song of a girl would follow. With a voice heavy as if under water:

"My love lies there,
In her beauty so rare,
In her coffin out under the daisies."

When the words had died mournfully away he would pat the keys lovingly, and shake his immense head slowly, chanting:

"Ah me—ah—my
Ah me—ah—my"

The climax came when he married Mrs. C. T. Yerkes, widow of the Chicago traction magnate. "I owned everything on wheels in Chicago," he bragged.

He was thirty. She was seventy.

After the marriage, he moved into her mansion of ornate red marble, full of paintings and tapestries.

His brother found him in a huge gilt bed made for the King of Bavaria. He was covered in the most delicate of point lace. He wore a red woolen undershirt, and a week's growth of beard. His servant was a bartender from a San Francisco saloon.

"It is very comfortable here, and the service is excellent," he explained.

The bartender pretended to be deaf and dumb to all in the mansion but Mizner. He was thus able to report to his master all that was said in the house.

So many complications arose that he was glad to get a divorce.

When asked upon what grounds, he answered, "Marriage is sufficient."

While in Germany he discovered a German who could make replicas of famous paintings. He brought him to America and opened a gallery on Fifth Avenue, calling it "The Old Masters."

"I started to devote my life to art—and sold reproductions for a hundred dollars each. A jobber from Boston offered me only fifty dollars for Da Vinci's 'Last Supper.' 'No, sir,' I told him, 'It's worth ten dollars a plate, and I'm only charging a hundred for the whole thing.' "

He became the manager of Stanley Ketchell, great middleweight pugilist. It was a weird combination.

Mizner paid no atention to the pugilist. The pugilist paid none to his training.

When he heard that Ketchell was on his death bed, he said, "Count ten over him—then he'll get up."

Ketchell's tragedy never left him. A man carved out of granite, flambuoyant, brutal, moody, with brilliant flashes, and courage to face a lion, the magnetic Ketchell was all the huge playboy wished to be. He would choke in revery.

"And killed with a Flobert rifle—over a hired hand's girl."

He once went to the mighty bruiser's grave. Standing over the weedy enclosure, he broke down and hurried away.

An atheist, he placed a Bible in the hands of a young suicide.

When a story he told to a film producer was rejected as having no audience appeal, he said scornfully, "The tale I just told you was *The Deep Purple*. It ran for two years on Broadway, and I wrote it."

His largest sale to the films was that of the wreck of the Titanic for twenty-five thousand dollars. His title was *God's Deal*.

His salary with a film company was five hundred dollars a week. "I'd work for them for nothing," he said, "just to have a place to go."

His chief value was in inventing trick situations on a level with his mediocre melodramas of an earlier day.

Like his literary god, O. Henry, he saw life through a small and tricky lens.

He scorned the millions who made up picture audiences. As an artist he was but slightly above them.

He would watch an ant trudge up a hill with a burden

greater than itself. The flight of a bee, the labor of a spider, made him pause in wonder and silence.

He would drive to the country each spring and gaze at orchards in bloom.

He stared at the mountains that encircled my home, his eyes dim, his mind full of never-to-be-answered questions, and said dolefully, "I will lift mine eyes unto the mountains whence cometh my strength."

The wittiest man in America, he but proved how ephemeral wit can be without the burning brain of a Swift behind it. And yet, there were times he might have walked with Swift.

An intense loneliness, tinged with a greater fear of death, came over him more acutely during the last year. Pursued by phantoms, he could not escape.

"Can't you take it standing up?" I asked him.

"Not if I can help it—I've been whistling in the dark all my life." He smiled dismally. "I'll soon be like Yorick —you can ask me all the damn fool questions—'Where be your gibes now? your gambols? your songs? your flashes of merriment, that were wont to set the table on a roar?' "

When the doctor brought the oxygen apparatus, the playboy said wearily, "It looks like the main event, Doc."

He did not move or speak again.

He was fifty-eight years old—the last of a magnificent school, that with him closed forever.

JIM CRUZE

JIM CRUZE

I first met him nearly thirty years ago. Hollywood was a charming town then. Everybody knew everybody else. One street, "the boulevard," along which the trolley cars jogged, ran lazily through it.

Avoiding the traps in which routine placed people, we did not consider what a lack of it meant in our lives. Hollywood was the gaudiest carnival in America. A suburb of Los Angeles, eight miles from a railroad, it had no established routine. We, the adventurers of the emotions, were happy in it. Each night we talked "shop" after wearing ourselves out during the day with toil to escape conventional work.

We were of all types. Jim Cruze was a Dane. Paul Bern was a Jew—with Jean Harlow far away. I was the roving son of an Irish ditch digger. Von Stroheim was an Austrian. Albert Lewin was a Russian. Al Green and Clarence Brown were Americans; Boris Karloff a truck driver who had been in college at Oxford, England. Harry Carey was from a town in New York. William S. Hart had traveled in Shakespeare. Tom Mix had been a cowboy in Texas.

The leading studio was the Paramount, organized by Jesse Lasky, a former cornet player. Though other studios were not in Hollywood, we made it our headquarters and were proud when "Variety" named it second to New York as the news centre of the nation. It was something to be "in pictures" then.

A DOZEN AND ONE

There was big news one evening. One of us, Lon Chaney, had electrified the nation as the star of a film and a master of cinematic make-up. The son of a deaf and dumb barber, he was our proof that we had a chance in life.

He and Jim Cruze were great friends. When Cruze congratulated him, he said, "Thanks, Jimmy. It's your turn next. Someday you'll hit—but never as an actor."

"Why?" Cruze asked.

"That's easy. You're too self-conscious," replied Chaney. "If you hang around railroad stations long enough, though, you can always tell those that are going places by lookin' at their eyes—and you've got exactly what it takes to make a director."

"I hope you're right," returned Cruze.

One of twenty-three children, Jim Cruze was heavily muscled, broad shouldered, six feet two and leonine. Simple as a child, he was complex as the riddle of life. The son of a three hundred pound Danish immigrant who settled in Utah as a follower of Brigham Young, his real name was Jens Bozen.

Born near Ogden, Utah, in 1884, he changed his name to Cruze and left home at fifteen to travel over the West with a medicine show. It was during these days while bumping over yellow leagues of desert that destiny prepared him for the man that was to be. With less than two years of academic schooling he had a good brain and quick apprehension.

Leaving the medicine show, he became a roustabout on a whaling vessel that took him to Japan. Returning to America, a stowaway, he became a road kid and eventually reached Alaska. That country's vast solitude impressed him. He stayed there for more than a year, then came to San Francisco.

Meeting Luke Cosgrave, who was a teacher of drama there, he was encouraged and financed by him as a student in a dramatic school. Somnolent as an Indian and resembling the romantic American conception of one, he drifted about the land as an actor in the roles of Red Men. Finding himself in New York, where existence as a stage actor was precarious, he secured the film lead in a serial called "The Million Dollar Mystery."

Hearing tales of Hollywood, he left for the film city. His name meant next to nothing. Soon destitute, he took a job as an extra player.

"I'd be on my way east, but Luke Cosgrave's coming here from Frisco," he said to me.

Luke Cosgrave brought hope with him. He had money and rented a shack.

Cruze told him what Chaney had said.

"He's right," Cosgrave returned. "You look like a million on the screen, but you can't act worth a cent."

Jim struggled eight years to become a director. Then

chance dropped a golden apple in his lap.

Jesse Lasky gave him Peter B. Kyne's "Valley of the Giants" to direct.

Peter looked at the daily "rushes" of the story.

"This fellow Cruze—who is he?" the writer asked Lasky. "He can paint with a camera far horizons that I can't describe."

Lasky remembered. A western story had been rejected by all his directors. He gave it to Cruze to read.

"I think it would make a good picture," Cruze handed it to me.

"How do you like it?" he said when I had finished. He watched the rain fall against the window of Luke's shack.

"It's your chance," I said. "It's got action and a theme."

His eyes danced. "Maybe Lon's right."

"Sure, he's right," I said. "You haven't got a thing to lose."

Luke Cosgrave added, "That's right—nothing to lose, and the world to gain."

We looked at the debonair Cosgrave, while the driven rain ran down the window.

Waiting for Lasky the next morning was Jim Cruze. His cap was awry, his shirt open, road kid fashion.

"I just read that story," he said stoically.

"I waited anxiously," said Lasky later. "I knew I

couldn't make him direct it, even if he was the least important director on the lot."

"Mr. Lasky," Cruze said, "will you let me direct that picture?"

"Can you feel it?" asked the incredulous Lasky.

"That's why I'm here," was the reply. "Besides I know the country it's laid in. I was born there."

"That so?" the future producer of "Sergeant York" said. "You can direct the film."

The director paced the floor. "Now one more thing. I'm the boss of my outfit," he said. "No relations to tell me what to do. Besides, Mr. Lasky, if the film hits I want mine."

"What'll yours be" asked Lasky.

"More'n a thousand dollars a day."

"That's a lot of money—but you'll be worth it," Lasky smiled, "if you make it hit big."

Walter Woods, a crack scenario writer, was engaged to work with Cruze. An excellent part was "built up" for Luke Cosgrave.

Jim Cruze had long admired Stephen Collins Foster —"The day goes by like a shadow o'er the heart." "I'll make that a theme song," he said.

Walter Woods ruled it out. "It's not box-office. Besides, wagons don't throw shadows over your heart."

Cruze arched his heavy shoulders. "Okay—how's this?

A DOZEN AND ONE

"It rained all night the day I left,
The weather it was dry,
The sun so hot I froze to death,
Susanna, don't you cry.
Oh, Susanna, don't you cry for me,
I've come from Alabama wid
My banjo on my knee."

Walter Woods listened. "That'll fit into wagons rolling west," he said.

It was the first of the great theme songs.

The story ready, all went on location. I stayed behind in Luke's shack to write.

The company soon faced a Utah winter. A blizzard cracked the pines. All were in despair. California and warmth were less than a thousand miles away.

"There's no use to wire the studio. I told Lasky that I was the boss of the outfit and that goes," Cruze said to Luke Cosgrave.

Standing on a stump of a pine tree in the midst of the windy desolation, the young director shouted to his gathering.

"This makes it hard for all of you, but don't forget it makes it a damn sight harder for me. There are two things we can do. One of them is to slip back to Hollywood and come here next summer and make this picture. The other is to stay right here and make it now. If any

140

of you want to stay, I'll stay with you, for, by God, I intend to stay anyhow."

A mighty shout came. "We'll stay, Jimmy."

For eight weeks Cruze shared every vicissitude with them.

The picture, "The Covered Wagon," was the first of the really geat epics that made millions.

When the contract was made, Lasky gave Cruze seven thousand and one dollars a week.

"What's the dollar for?" asked Cruze.

"You said you had to have more than a thousand dollars a day—I remember," said Lasky.

"You're a damned square man," exploded the director.

"No—I just have a good memory," returned Lasky.

Cruze bought a mansion and called it his road house. His name soon became a monstrous legend.

He took ten men to a tailor shop. "A hundred and fifty a suit's your limit," he said.

"I kin git a home for that out where I live," an extra player grinned.

He bought his Danish mother a fig orchard and sent men to give her exorbitant prices for ordinary figs. One man offered her a large sum for the orchard. She asked her son's advice.

"I wouldn't sell it—not when you get so much for your figs."

He kissed her white hair.

Elmer Ellsworth was always near. "I get more laughs with him," the taciturn sentimentalist said.

His house was filled with dark servants. His guests were requested to say nothing racial. "It's bad enough to have to work for me. No use to go out of our way to hurt their feelings."

Men were not encouraged to give their seats to ladies in his mansion. "If she's a strong enough lady, she can find a seat for herself."

He seldom removed his cap. "I think he sleeps in it," said Ellsworth.

There was about him a monstrous dignity. Though casual and carefree, one would as soon have slapped God on the back. And yet, the hurt lad shivering with the fare-thee-wells, found a ready listener in him.

When I told him of John Gay's lines, he asked me to write them for him—

"Life is a jest; and all things show it.
I thought so once; but now I know it."

He had them framed and placed in his room.

When I described George Jean Nathan's abhorrence of films, he said, "I don't like oatmeal for breakfast—so what!"

"But you'd like Nathan," I said, "and he'd like you."

He filled his glass. "How do you know?"

"Because he likes the genuine."

JIM CRUZE

He lifted his glass. "That's different."

Lasky next brought a lanky fellow to him. Cruze wrote and directed a film for him and called it "One Glorious Day." Imbued with Cruze's personality, it is still a classic. The lanky fellow was Will Rogers.

There was a sign above Cruze's gate—"Beware of the dog." Once inside, a gentle toy bulldog came.

Cruze's most memorable day was in entertaining H. L. Mencken. Several hundred people attended. He met Mincken at the door and said, "I'm Jim Cruze and I've never read a God damn thing you ever wrote."

And Mencken returned, "Well, I never saw one of your God damn pictures—that makes us both Elks."

The editor was soon surrounded by the Hollywood beauty of Hedda Hopper, Ruth Chatterton, Irene Rich, Aileen Pringle and Betty Compson.

Thinking of his home city, as usual, he said, "When I was a youngster in Baltimore the girls in the sporting houses called me professor."

Betty Compson looked coyly at him, "I thought your face was familiar," she said.

Cruze spilled his drink with laughter.

When it came time to go home, the chauffeur, who had brought Joseph Hergesheimer and Aileen Pringle in her town car, was intoxicated. Mencken decided to go home with them. After nearly dumping the occupants of the car in a canyon, Hergesheimer got out and spoke shaarply to him.

"Listen, you son of a bitch—you can't talk to me that way," the chauffeur replied.

A compromise was reached, when Hergesheimer and Mencken placed the chauffeur between them, while Miss Pringle drove the town car the twenty miles home.

In honor of my appearance in the fiftieth magazine, a dinner was given by Betty Compson, Mrs. James Cruze.

"We are being entertained," I looked at Betty, "by the most beautiful girl who ever came to Hollywood. She has one other distinction—that of being the only cinema queen with an international reputation who ever went to high school."

Loaded with gin, Cruze went to his room. "I'm going to die tonight," he said.

We waited for his end. The lightning flared above Mount Wilson.

"That's Jimmy's soul," Betty Compson said.

The next day I telephoned at noon.

"What the hell's eating you—calling a guy so early in the morning. Come on out here."

Two days before I had given him a play to read, upon which I had collaborated with Frank Dazey. It concerned a simple Negro giant pugilist's moral and physical disintegration. Called "Black Boy," it later starred Paul Robeson in New York.

When I arrived, he was sitting bent over, his elbows on his knees. I asked his opinion of it. He rose, shook his head and said, "God, what you boys did to that big, beautiful man."

Warner Oland stepped out of a powerful car, followed by a scenario writer in riding boots. Cruze said to the scenarist, "Gee, if you ever get to where you are now, you'll be terrific."

The Oriental quality in Oland, the brilliant Swede who translated and introduced Stringberg to America, and ended as Charlie Chan, the Chinese detective, mystified him greatly.

"You're a Swede who looks like a Chinaman, and I'm a Dane who looks like an Indian."

Motion pictures were his only interest . . . Frank Moran was the best unrecognized film comedian in Hollywood; Mal St. Clair had the finest touch among the younger directors; Frank Capra and John Ford were good men at the megaphone. He was fond of Tom Mix and Harry Carey. "They're more'n cowboys," he said.

Though he claimed that he only read material that made films, he knew Schopenhauer.

"Where did you read him?" I asked.

"On the road, as a kid," he replied. "The old devil just got in under the wire. Pointing to his hair, Schopenhauer said of his late fame 'Time has brought his roses at last, but they are white.' " Cruze hunched his shoulders, "Very lovely."

His apprehension never lagged.

"Are you with me?" asked the teller of a tale.

"I'm ahead of you," was the answer.

He would seldom leave his mansion without taking his own gin.

"Drinking strange liquor ruins a guy's health."

Renee Adoree, the lovely star of "The Big Parade," was ill in a Hollywood hospital.

"He'll go to see Renee," said Betty Compson. "He'd even miss a drink to call on a pal in pain."

He was said to have helped make Renee a film star. His eyes were less quizzical when her name was mentioned.

In a short time Archie, the chauffeur, appeared with the limousine, and a full bottle. We called on Renee.

"Take your cap off, Jimmy," said Betty.

"What for? It's windy in here," replied her husband.

He was diffident in the surroundings. On leaving, he said, "I'll be seein' you, Renee. So long."

He was in one of his mystifying silences all the way home.

Cruze was married three times. His first wife was Marguerite Snow, an actress, and the mother of his daughter, Julie.

One Sunday as Julie played the piano, he asked my opinion.

"Tin Pan Alley," I walked away.

"I'm afraid so," he looked at the group around the piano, then followed me.

His second wife was Betty Compson.

His third was not of "the profession."

Having directed the epic of land, and not liking the sea, he was given "Old Ironsides" to direct. He called it "Old I-ron'-si-dées."

We talked of Alaska on location. He told of a thresher whale in the northern waters that got caught in a net and tore it to pieces. He looked mirthlessly at the peaceful sea.

"Up in that country," he said, "there's a pack of wolves that run all night. They're all friendly with one another until one of them shows the least sign of blood; then the rest devour it and go right on. That's Hollywood."

"You mean it's life," I retorted. "I get tired of hearing the place abused—as though people were different here."

His eyes were on me. *"That* coming from you!" he said.

"Sure, why not? We couldn't fit in anywhere else," I said. He started to move away. "A fellow like you talking about wolves. You're wrong as hell. No one here asked you to throw your life away. You're a greatly gifted man, Jimmy—a Beethoven in a honky-tonk. No history of the films would be complete without a chapter on you. You've directed at least two masterpieces and you're still the greatest director in Hollywood. You owe so much to yourself—you'd have been a success even if there hadn't been pictures to direct."

"At what, for instance, Mr. Jarnegan?"

I had written a novel of a Hollywood director.

"Don't make him like me," he had advised.

Heeding Cruze, I gave him a different background and Danton's description.

"We must dare and again dare, and forever dare," Danton had shouted.

"Jarnegan was like Danton—he didn't quit—I like guys who don't talk of wolves."

Cruze turned. "Jarnegan didn't have sense enough to quit. It was always the third act in a melodrama with him—and you pinned him on me."

"He *was* you," I put in.

"Are you kiddin'?" he said. "Jarnegan was *you*—if you were a director like me." He smiled.

"A great director—like you," I answered.

He snapped his fingers, "Oh, nuts—we can't quit now. Remember the days when we struggled like hell—and for what the little boy shot at. Let's go."

His huge room had five gallons of gin and a dainty miniature of Betty Compson.

He went through the motions of directing the film in

148

the morning. Still the "fastest director" in Hollywood, his eyes took in everything. No scene was taken over twice. This film, like his others ,was finished ahead of schedule.

Under another director than Cruze, "Old Ironsides" might have passed unnoticed. But so much was expected of him. It was his first great failure. Not knowing that he might be a thresher whale, he was handled severely by the critics.

Word went around that he had slipped. "He can't drink gin at Flintridge and let the world go by," a producer said. His option was dropped.

Such men as George Kauffman, Marc Connelly, Carl Van Vechten and Lawrence Stallings were still fascinated by him.

A new company had formed. He was offered three thousand dollars a week. A lesser salary than a thousand dollars a day was unthinkable. To save his pride he became a producer. Erich von Stroheim became the star of Cruze's first film, "The Great Gabbo."

Capable of earning two hundred thousand dollars a year, Stroheim owed for the furniture in a four room flat.

"I admire his nerve and damn his judgment," the embryo artist said, "but he's got as much as I have." He recalled the old days. "Stroheim never merely entered a room—he made an entrance."

Cruze liked Stroheim. He had succeeded after Chaney. As an extra player he had sold Uncle Carl

Laemmle, head of Universal City, the idea of a film about a man who had faith in a woman.

"What'll we call it?" Uncle Carl had asked.

"The Pinnacle" or "Blind Husbands," replied Stroheim.

"We'd better call it "Blind Husbands," Uncle Carl grinned. "There's more of them than pinnacles."

The film had made Stroheim famous.

"Those were the happy days," said Cruze. "I see Chaney's hit again." His eyes had a faraway look. "The old gang's all gone places. Al Green and Clarence Brown are now big directors. Albert Lewin and Paul Bern are with Thalberg. Boris Karloff's following Lon Chaney. Harry Carey and Tom Mix are still going. They have taught cowboys to ride—no doubles for them." He smiled. "Dear old Bill Hart—two gun Othello. All of them were swell guys." He sighed. "They put Hollywood on the map."

When "The Great Gabbo" was previewed, Cruze said to me, "Something's wrong."

"Yes, Jimmy, it's not fundamental enough. Nobody cares what happens to a lot of cake eaters."

"Don't rub it in," he said.

"I'm not, Jimmy. This is a good film. *But it's not you.* 'The Covered Wagon' was."

"I know," his voice was low.

On our way to his estate, the engine of a freight whistled.

"Highballin' to Bakersfield. I hope no poor bum's on it."

Cruze looked out. The lights of his limousine darted across a hobo.

"Stop the car, Archie," Cruze said. "Want a ride, mister?" he asked.

Scared, the man got in.

"Which way?" asked Cruze.

"Los Angeles."

"That's just where we're going," he lied. "Didya eat yet? Here's a ten spot."

"Thanks, mister," the vagrant said.

"My name's Joe Doakes," Cruze looked at me, "and this fellow's name's Jesse Lasky."

"Pleased to meet you, Mr. Lasky."

The man left the car in front of a Main Street dive.

Passing a group getting a film star's autograph, Cruze grinned, "She'll be forgotten before they get home with her name."

He was silent all the way home.

Our ways soon diverged. There needs be no blame here. I would do it differently now. I was younger then.

"We each owe the other three thousand dollars, Jimmy," I said.

"Mine's on a different deal," he looked at his desk.

"All right, Jimmy," I handed him my check and walked out of his office forever.

"Two tramps quarreling over money." His words followed me.

The years passed. The old longing came. I would drive out to see him soon.

Then we read that each had a heart attack.

To my ranch twenty-five miles away came a car driven by Mrs. Elmer Ellsworth, a woman beyond seventy.

"Jimmy wants to see you," she said. "I'll take you to him and bring you back."

Touched by the magnanimous offer, I returned, "I'll send Jimmy a note that I'll go to see him tomorrow." I looked at her strong face. "You've been Jimmy's friend a long time."

Her eyes went over the far fields. "No one ever leaves Jimmy," she said.

I went to see him the next day.

"Myrtle," I said to my wife of some years, "this is Jim Cruze."

"Your name 'Myrtle'?" he asked.

She nodded.

"And you've never done anything about it?" he asked.

The room was crowded with the heterogeneous col-

lection of a fellow who has lived much. Nearby was the
marble bust of a gladiator with a broken nose.

"Supposed to be from the ruins of Pompeii," I remembered.

A small and not remarkable Rembrandt was sunk
deep in a ten inch frame.

"Who did the frame, Jimmy? It's a masterpiece."

"It was made on the set. I told the guy what I
wanted."

Above his bed, "large as a ham actor's opinion of
himself," was an original Memling.

"Rember the time you took your own gin to Europe?"
I laughed.

"Yeap—and came back with that damned painting—
the face looks like an egg a school kid put eyes on."

His eyes went to the chap with the broken nose.

"He's seen a lot since he came from Italy—if he could
only talk!" I said.

"It's a good thing he can't," Cruze returned faintly.

His wife straightened the covers.

"I'll be leaving now—so long, Jimmy." I turned to
his wife. "There's greatness in this big Dane you married."

He was on my mind for two days. In San Francisco
I learned that he had died.

Luke Cosgrave, beyond eighty, made a last talk over
his one time brilliant pupil.

A DOZEN AND ONE

Following cremation, his ashes were placed next to Renee Adoree's.

"I'll be seein' you," he had told the beautiful star of "The Big Parade."

ARNOLD BENNETT

ARNOLD BENNETT

We had exchanged several letters in London. He wrote warmly of my work which had appeared in *Vanity Fair*, but made no mention of my books. My interview with him was set eight days in advance. On the scheduled day I received a letter from him saying that he only talked for the annoyance of his friends. He thus placed me on my honor not to quote him.

Wondering who had warned him against me, I smiled and kept the appointment.

He lived in a grimy four story building which overlooked Cadogan Square. All the roofs in his neighborhood were fringed with chimney pots. A small stretch of lawn was at the rear of his house.

A man servant led me through the hall to a staircase. The hall was crowded with the possessions of a man of exquisite taste.

I entered a panelled Georgian room with a parquetry floor. Bowls of flowers were all about. A rich green was used in the furnishings. Fine paintings were in profusion.

The door of the room opened suddenly. Arnold Bennett stood at attention. His movement had been that of an immense mannequin. His hand went to his forehead in a kind of a salute. He stood against the wall for a moment. I introduced the lady with me. He bowed stiffly; then turned from her and greeted me even more stiffly.

He was as wide as Rodin's statue of Balzac. Not exactly fat, his round, heavy-set figure was expansive. His hair, gray and thick, stood, hedgelike, from the top of his head. His eyes were vivid and sad. His mouth was large, his lips thick, his teeth far above the average size. Through his florid face ran tiny purple streaks. With a hand, heavy as a peasant's, he felt often his close-cropped moustache. He held his head backward. I divided my attention between his mouth and his eyes. His mouth was generous, coarse, and sensuous, the mouth of a man whose passions would not be too fastidious.

He wore a checkered suit, a red necktie, and a salmon-colored silk shirt.

Younger English writers had affectionately called him A.B. I wanted very much to like him.

He had a hesitancy in his speech.

In the middle of a sentence he would throw his head back, close his eyes, and open his cavernous mouth.

All would become silent. Finally the most important word in the sentence would come out like the crack of a whip.

H. G. Wells told me that Bennett could have corrected the impediment in his speech had he so desired.

The sentence completed, Bennett would immediately assume the attitude of a man in a room with a tiger that might at any moment mutilate his many paintings and destroy his bric-a-brac.

His aloofness made me doubt his capacity for catching the feelings of others. His breeding was not sufficient to enable him to meet me on common ground.

I recalled to myself that he had somewhere written, "People have said to me: 'But you are so critical. You condemn everything.' Such is the complaint of laity against the person who has diligently practiced the cultivation of his taste. And, roughly speaking, it is a well-founded and excusable complaint. A person of fine taste does condemn nearly everything."

I tried to fit his words with his appearance while he talked to the lady with me. Wrinkles of interest came to the edges of his complacent eyes, while I gazed at a painting of two bitter old curmudgeons huddled in a cab.

It was a picture taken out of nature. A brutal, cunning old man sat hunched in the seat, his tenacious hands clasped. His lips were puckered as though a thorn were in his throat. Wrinkles ran between his eyes and down his withered neck. Near him was a senile, abject woman.

"I like that picture," I volunteered.

Bennett's stiff body loosened.

"That's my treasure," he said. His guard went up again. He looked about the room as if to make sure that no object were missing.

The lady with me sat, a cigarette in her hand, her dress to her knees. The eyes of the great writer discovered her leg. They did not move for some time.

A child could be heard wailing.

"Have you children?" he asked the lady.

"No," she answered.

"They're a nuisance," he said.

"And your ambition?" he asked her.

"To be a writer."

The successful novelist shrugged his shoulders, "Two writers in one house—good God!" A frown went over his heavy face. His head tilted back, his mouth went open, his eyes closed.

Dreading the long pause, I asked, "Are you coming to America soon, Mr. Bennett?"

"Not soon, if ever," he half choked. "Club women drinking tea," he hesitated again, "My God!"

His eyes opened in painful memory. The purple streaks widened in his face.

He rose and poured tea. His hand fumbled with the silver sugar tongs.

I refused the yellow concoction.

He had told me in a letter that he owned the best Bourbon in London.

He pressed a button. A servant entered with glasses.

"It's too bad there's prohibition in America," he said.

"I haven't noticed it," I said.

He looked at me, not unkindly. His thick lips curved in a smile.

"Is the *Life of Henry VIII* still selling well over there?" he asked, almost with banter.

"Oh yes," I answered, "We're all bigamists at heart—Henry's our hero."

He shook his head at the riddle of our benighted nation.

The talk drifted to American writers.

He was none too fond of Dreiser, but admired greatly the work of Sinclair Lewis.

"He doesn't carry as much water as Dreiser," I said.

He got my meaning. His head again went back. His mouth opened. He said nothing.

The hubbub created by Mrs. Sinclair Lewis' trouble with Dreiser had but recently pased. He was sure that Dreiser was big enough to go it alone without a woman journalist's idea of Russia. "Both writers may have obtained their material from the same sources," he said.

He admired Douglas Fairbanks. "A ham actor who can jump," was my comment. He returned to his idol three times.

"He can still jump," I agreed.

He made it final with, "An unusual fellow."

We came to Hemingway. "I have read him in French," he said, triumphantly.

George Bernard Shaw's name was mentioned. "He is our circus," he said.

"More than that," I put in.

"Oh yes, far more." I felt that he was fond of Shaw.

The talk drifted to a young English writer who had

so devotedly called Bennett A.B. "He will never arrive at his destination," said Bennett. His head went back. There was fully a minute's pause between stutters, then he finished, "He is just a fool—an intellectual fool." The description was deadly accurate. The man from the Five Towns knew how to read a fool.

"There are many of them in America," I said.

His head tilted back, his mouth opened for an endless half minute, and he said, "I have met them," his head went further back, "all." He finished with a mighty effort.

His interest in American prisons recalled his humble beginnings. As I talked of life's stragglers, I had, for a few minutes, the great author of THE OLD WIVES' TALE for a listener. Gone was the snob and the libertine. In his place was all that will make Arnold Bennett immortal—his pity for the defeated and the despised.

The lady with me moved in her seat. Arnold Bennett took another glance at her silk clad leg.

He asked me which English writer had impressed me most. I answered, "Thomas Hardy." His eyes opened a trifle wider. Hardy had but recently died. "His books are now selling well in America," I said.

Bennett's head went further back. He opened his mouth and stammered for a full minute, then said bluntly, "His death helped him."

The young lady tapped the end of a cigarette. The

great man struck a match, rose stiffly, and leaned over the lady.

Vermeer would have enjoyed the picture. The delicate face of the girl, puffing the cigarette, while the light from the match in the London dusk accentuated the strong florid features of the great writer who had risen from despair.

He had started in London as a clerk at twenty-five shillings a week. A fourth of that amount went for a small bedroom.

In ten years he rode the high waves of success. if he wore that success like a traveling salesman, it must be remembered that there was much insular mud in his make-up.

His undershot jaw was proof that the futility of all things human concerned him not at all. A heavy moth with a good brain, he flew to every social occasion.

Sure of himself always among his inferiors, he could still be surprised when Henry James treated him as an equal.

His taste was more feminine than masculine. If he soared a few times like an eagle, it was the tail of the peacock that pulled him down.

He wrote of himself and his possessions in the manner of a Cockney with his first new suit of clothes.

That he was one of the Lords of literature in London

chiefly for the lack of bigger and braver men, he was
evidently not aware.

He had long ago honestly admitted that he took up
writing to earn a living. He had written nearly a quarter
of a million words in a year—a tremendous output, even
for a man built like a heavyweight bruiser.

In middle life, he wrote of himself:

"The curtain rises on the figure of an editor, novelist,
dramatist, critic, connoisseur of all arts. See him in his
suburban residence, with its poplar-shaded garden, its
bicycle-house at the extremity thereof, and its horizon
composed of the District Railway Line. See the study,
lined with two thousand books, garnished with photo-
gravures, and furnished with a writing bureau and a chair
and nothing else. See the drawing-room with its artistic
wall-paper, its Kelmscotts, its water-colors of a palid but
indubitable distinction, its grand piano on which are a
Wagnerian score and Bach's Two-part Inventions. See
the bachelor's bedroom, so austere and precise, wherein
Boswell's 'Johnson' and Baudelaire's'Fleurs du Mal' exist
peaceably together on the night-table. The entire machine
speaks with one voice, and it tells you that there are no
flies on that young man, that that young man never
gives the wrong change. He is in the movement, he is
correct; but at the same time he is not so simple as not
to smile with contemptuous toleration at all movements
and all correctness. He knows. He is a complete guide to

art and life. His innocent foible is never to be at a loss, and never to be carried away—save now and then, because an occasional ecstasy is good for the soul."

And yet, this brave fellow whose innocent foible was never to be at a loss, and who was a complete guide to art and life, was afraid to let himself be quoted by an American hobo.

His wife returned as we were leaving. Much younger than Bennett, vivacious and effervescent, she uttered the usual polite banalities. She was deeply sorry not to have been able to seize on the great opportunity of meeting me. She only had eight days in which to prepare.

I glanced at Bennett.

The most famous citizen of Five Towns was more like blubber than mannequin now. Swiftly and apologetically he had aged. The stiffness had gone from the social lion's tail. His lips moved in never-to-be-heard whispers.

As one walks out of a room of death, I moved toward the door.

The two women were chattering. Arnold Bennett came toward me.

We shook hands without a word.

I looked straight in his eyes.

They dropped, to hide his soul.

He put his arm around me.

His head was still forward. There was no stammer now.

"I will read your books," he said.

More than a year passed. He praised highly the worst book ever written about American hoboes.

Frank Swinnerton read his comment and asked him in a London newspaper if he had ever read Jim Tully's *Beggars of Life*.

The great libertine from the Five Towns did not answer.

TOD SLOAN

TOD SLOAN

There was in him the vanity of a little man. Immaculate, poised, well-tailored, his head was much larger in proportion than the rest of his body. His step was short, and springy. Not over five feet tall, his magnificent presence came from an innate mastery of horses and men. His emotions, never easily touched, made his friendship valuable. His words, always cryptic, were not many.

His hands were small, and as firmly put together as leaden mallets. His body was well muscled, taut and under control.

He might have been all the jockeys in the world going down the track after the race is won.

He smoked a dozen strong black cigars in a day. Abstemious with food, he would drink copiously of beer or other highly fattening liquids. He would indulge in stronger liquor by the hour and walk without a stagger.

His temperament, keyed to a high pitch, was always the same. Even in liquor he did not become loquacious.

An inveterate gambler, he would have staked his life on the turn of a card, and have faced a firing squad with eyes unbandaged.

Great through force of character, the race track was his expression. An expert in all things that required control, Tod Sloan could handle a gun like Daniel Boone, a billiard cue easily as Willie Hoppe, and the reigns of a fractious horse like God.

He was born in Indiana over sixty-five years ago.

A DOZEN AND ONE

His father, a violin-playing barber in Kokomo, had been a sergeant in the Union Army during the Civil War.

Named James Foreman Sloan at birth, he was later called Toad because of his small size.

He soon called himself J. Todhunter Sloan. It was shortened to Tod when he became the greatest jockey of all recorded time.

He early developed sardonic penetration. With but little sentiment and no sentimentality, he liked dogs and horses.

"I talked *with them*—not to them."

His mother died when he was five years old. He had two brothers, Cassius and Fremont.

On Saturday he would stand on a stool and lather faces in his father's barber shop.

During the week, he would remain away from school and wander around with "my only close friend, a mongrel dog by the name of Tony."

He had found Tony on a country road.

Each morning his father sent him to the home of Pat Grace to get a can of milk. Grace had a huge bull dog.

Tod and the bull dog developed a warm friendship. "One morning Tony followed me to Grace's home. The bull dog grabbed Tony's throat. Unable to loosen him, I took a knife and stabbed him to the heart."

He went to Pat Grace.

" 'I've killed your dog,' I said. He never spoke to me again."

Several in the neighborhood wanted to send Tod to a reform school. "I had a 'bad reputation' anyhow. I was thirteen and smoked a pipe."

Frightened, he ran away with Tony to his aunt's. She asked Tod sarcastically if he had brought his trunk.

"I had no trunk, so I took the hint." He got a job in the oil fields, where an explosion burnt him so badly he had to remain in limewater for two months.

"I was so little I was in the way of everything but the explosion."

His elder brother Cassius was the next to leave home. "He had a fight with Dad, and lit out down the railroad track, the old man after him. It was Cash's first race, and he won it."

Cash found work with a stable of horses at the Fair Grounds. Tod worked with him a few weeks.

Tod was afraid of horses. "My one experience hadn't ended so good. Borrowing a livery horse, without the owner's consent, I got on its back. Scared as I was, the horse ran away. I couldn't get off the damn thing till a man caught it. Just to show I was not afraid, he wanted me to ride it back to the livery stable. It was my turn to run."

He next worked as a "clean-up" boy in a Kokomo saloon until his prohibitionist father objected.

Deprived of this livelihood, he joined "Professor" Talbot, who made balloon ascensions, ran side shows, and other make-shifts so common to a carnival grifter.

With a dollar of the professor's money, he saw a man operating a shell game.

"Now you see it, now you don't," said the man. Fascinated, the boy watched the three shells and the pea. "I bet the dollar it was under the wrong shell and lost," he told the professor.

"The professor went to the man who ran the game and told him not to cheat one of his own gang." He returned the money.

The professor who had never seen a parachute, made one from a picture. In a few days he advertised that he was going to throw his "little boy" out of the balloon in a parachute. He was to get twenty-five dollars for the act.

"Who is your little boy," Tod asked.

"You are, son," said the Professor.

"The hell I am," exclaimed Tod.

The fifteen-year-old boy went to work—"around the horses" with his brother, Cash.

He made his first appearance on a horse in a few months. "I was supposed to merely walk it around the track. When it broke into a run, the stable boys came after me. Figuring it was a real race, the horse did a half mile in thirteen seconds. That would of been all right, but he stopped sudden and threw me over his head."

It was decided then that Tod would never be a jockey. He was given work in the kitchen.

After several months he again attempted to ride, without success.

"A saying got around the tracks, that if a man didn't want his horse to win, just let me ride him. That was handicap enough."

Then something happened.

While galloping his horse to the post, it started to bolt. In trying to pull him in, Tod "got out of the saddle and up on the horse's neck." The stride of his horse was more free and the riding easier. "I began to practice this position in private. One day, when I tried it in public, the stands roared with laughter, thinking I was clowning. But I began to win races." It was the "monkey-on-a-stick" method that made him famous.

He next observed the advantage of "pocketing" in racing. Keeping his mount directly behind a group of horses, he let them serve as wind breakers. This not only cut down the resistance of the air but allowed the horse to breathe more easily. When the time came for a spurt to finish the race, Tod's pocketed horse was fresher than those leading. "I simply went between them for the short distance spurt."

He also learned that however tired a horse may be that given a chance to go between two horses or another

173

horse and the rail, it would take on new energy for a short distance. It won him many races.

Critics attributed his success to brains and hands. "They should of said heart too—one horse trusted me so much he would eat anything so long as he saw me take a bite first. I even had him eating sour oranges."

He became a protégé of Pittsburgh Phil Smith. One of the colorful men of his era, a cork-cutter who quit a dollar and a quarter a day job to follow horse racing, Smith ended worth five million dollars.

"He would back every mount I rode. I argued that a man was bound to lose betting like that." He grinned, "Never mind that—look at the fun I have. If I lose on you today, I'll bet like hell on you tomorrow."

No longer a stable roustabout, but a world famous jockey, Tod next joined the W. C. Whitney stables as star rider.

"After winning the Futurity race, Mr. Whitney called me aside. Pulling a couple of grand out of his pockets, he handed them to me. When I lost the money on the stock market, he scolded me for gambling, then gave me a tip that brought me over thirty thousand dollars."

Returning to Kokomo as a hero, he discovered that there was to be a ball at Logansport. Scores of citizens wanted to go, but had no way to get there. He ordered a special train and invited "the whole town to take a ride to Logansport." A hotel was "thrown open." In the middle of this lavish entertainment, he sent the special away. When his guests protested, "I told them I hadn't bought the train, that they could get home on the regular one."

Remembering the aunt who had so long ago asked him about his trunk, he invited her to visit him in New York.

She had never been more than sixty miles from home.

"I decided to ride for her benefit. After the third race I went to see how she was getting along.

" 'Just fine,' " she said, 'but when do you perform?'

"I told her I had already performed to the extent of winning two out of three races.

" 'Oh, that little fellow out in front—was that you? I saw some horses go by.'

" 'I told her to watch for my colors the next time. She did and I lost."

"I couldn't see that jacket of yours; you weren't performing in front that time?" said his aunt.

" 'No, it was a friend of mine's turn,' " I told her.

Skeets Martin, Lester and Johnny Reiff, his brother Cash, all Indiana jockeys, were riding in Europe. Tod became anxious to join them.

With a dozen trunks and a valet he went to England to ride for Lord Beresford. "I got my first win from a starting machine. It was still new over there."

Beating the barrier he covered nearly a quarter of the

distance before the other horses got started.

In dismay at the unexpected result the racing officials did not again use the machine for some time.

After an injury, he was unable to ride for two months.

Regaining the saddle, he won twenty-two races out of forty-eight starts. In the next two years the intrepid little strategist was to make a record never to be approached, "four winners a day for the next fifty days."

Golden apples fell from the trees in the sky. He had his shoes made—a dozen pairs at a time. As his size was but one and a half, he would offer a pair to any lady who could wear them.

He denied having taken eighteen trunks when he traveled. "Never over a dozen." His smile was poignant. "Why—I travel with fifty-three pieces now—a deck of cards and a necktie—and no one says anything."

When introduced to the Prince of Wales he did not remove his jockey cap.

"I didn't want to go to the dressing room to comb my hair," he explained.

Chosen to ride a horse for him, Tod advised the Prince to bet on the mount. Though a lord questioned his advice, the Prince bet six hundred pounds.

"I had to ride like hell, but I came in first."

He was presented with a special set of the royal stable's colors—with a diamond horse and jockey pin.

"I had forty thousand dollars worth of jewelry—so

this was one more piece," he said with wry whimsy. "It must of been worth two pounds—and from a guy who won six hundred, and was to be king of England at that."

"Did you like the Prince?" I asked.

"Oh, so so—he was a big pleasant fellow with a heavy gutteral voice."

I had never before heard him use so large a word as *gutteral*.

Unsurpassed as a rider, in courage he had no equal.

Jerked from a horse his head struck the ground; his ear drum burst. Refusing all entreaties to go to a hospital, he won the most important race that day.

He admired nerve in horses.

"Ridin' Holocaust in the English Derby, I'd come up from behind to take the lead—when his hoof snapped off —he run about six hundred feet on three legs. When the other horses shot past I crawled off, and there was the poor devil—his bleedin' stump stickin' in the ground. Right in sight of winnin' the greatest race on earth he turned to munch grass at the edge of the track. *He was a thoroughbred all the way—but dammit—I wanted to win that race.*"

"Suppose you'd been thrown off?"

"Well," he said, "It's not best to be in the lead if you lose your horse—you might get your brains tramped out."

"Do many riders go that way?"

"Not so many. If a jockey just lies still the chances

of a horse's hoofs grindin' into him's not so big as when he gets up and tries to run off the tracks. It's then he gets the works."

He listened as if for the rush of running horses.

His brother Cash might have been the world's great jockey—had Tod not been riding.

When he returned from being chief rider for the Czar of Russia, and visited Tod in England, the younger brother secured a good mount for him.

They talked back and forth on the track.

The race started. Cash came second.

"Sorry, Cash. I'd have given anything to see you win."

"Why the hell didn't you let me then?" was the question.

The finale of his brilliant career left a cloud of bitterness.

"I was ridin' a horse named "Cadoman" in the Cambridgeshire, an important English race. I bet heavily on myself and was also promised a handsome present if I should win." The horse came in second. "I was later called before the Stewards of the Jockey Club to account for my betting and intention of accepting a present. I admitted both, and explained that they were permitted in America."

Thirty years later he said, "It was a dirty frame-up. They couldn't think up ways to beat me—so they ruled me off."

To banish the horses of hateful memory, I said, "You can still ride any horse that ever ran."

"Or flew, by God," he added.

Bitter as rain, the Napoleon of horses without his saddle, he left England in 1900.

The shell of his life still hard, he took all things in their stride. Never phlegmatic, he was imperturbable.

The pity was that his grief had no outlet. "The rain fell in buckets."

He knew only the tracks and the muddy water upon them. There was no strong hand at the moment to guide the boy who could guide a thoroughbred stallion. "My heart was cracked. I'd of rather been kicked in the head." Not knowing how to break and pull himself together again, he suffered like a giant.

The history of a comrade's cupidity must be written with a colder hand than mine. Admitting his faults, I would cover them with weeds of wind-blown understanding.

His passion for gambling was the one horse he could not control. Once again the lad who had bet another man's dollar on a shell game, he won, lost, and won a fortune—at Monte Carlo.

Fiercely proud, he returned to America.

To love, except of himself, a swaggering and sardonic little stranger, the able introvert married Julia Sanderson, a talented and beautiful musical comedy star. "It was one of those things," he said. Julia undoubtedly felt the same way.

"You won't live with that guy a year," a theatrical producer said, and added grimly, "unless you're a horse."

"I'll bet you a kiss," said Julia.

"It's on," he grunted.

Several months later the producer was on a Broadway corner.

Out of a taxi came a lovely young woman. She kissed the producer, said "There," and hurried to the taxi.

Tod's next venture was opening a billiard room with John McGraw, manager of the New York Giants' Baseball Team.

Young Griffo, the greatest boxer that ever lived, was an habitué of the place.

Both early waifs, there was a kinship between the two greatest of their kind.

"Griffo was a favorite, but always broke," said Tod, not adding he had given him over ten thousand dollars.

"Those who listened to him, were usually asked to shell out some money before they parted company. One day he shook hands with an English visitor. 'By the way,' says Griffo—'Could you lend me a buck before you go?' 'Certainly,' said the visitor, 'How much is a buck?' 'Twenty dollars,' answered young Griffo.' "

At Griffo's suggestion Tod became a fight promotor. "One day a negro came to me with a letter from George

Considine asking that I give him a chance in the ring. I asked him if he could fight. His chest swelled, 'Yes suh, Mistah Sloan—I kin fight till de cows come home.' "

A fight was arranged. The negro was punched severely. At the end of the fourth round, to encourage him, Sloan said the other man was licked, that he wanted to call it a draw already. "For gawd's sake, tell him it's O.K. with me," said the negro. "What's the matter," asked Tod. "I thought you said you could fight till the cows come home." "I did, Mistah Sloan, but I done seen dem cows a-comin' when he hit me dat las' time."

After years of whistling at the canker of the past, he was still a king without his kingdom. He loved the clashing of hoofs as Beethoven the thunder of music.

His smile became a pucker, his heart heavy. The appetites encouraged in days of riches, were not so easily appeased.

Other jockeys might "follow the horses."

He could not be a tout.

Doddering into sensility, he lived over again the days of his dashing glory. His interests were confined to staccato memories.

For some years he studied horses, tracks and riders.

"So and so can't crawl in the mud"—or, "He runs with his heart and likes the heavy going."

Then the names of jockeys and horses became vague as those of great writers to scenarists. He put them all aside.

I brought to him a lad who had won a famous race at Santa Anita. Hot as wine with his victory, he stood before the king. When he had gone Tod said, "What was his name again, Jim?"

Talking of horses often, I told him a tale I had written of the Milky Way.

"It's made by Indians on horses chasing buffalo—they never quite catch up with them. That's what makes all the white dust."

"Huh, no damn Indian ever could ride a horse." He had never been aware of the sky. He almost glanced upward.

Living on a hill in Hollywood, he would walk slowly down to meet me each afternoon. Always, with a huge cigar and liquor, he would stay until weariness overtook him.

I would then send him home in a taxi.

His last illness was not long. He lay, the slightly gray hair going back from his immense forehead, his jaw still firm though battered with years, his eyes vivid and worn by pain, staring far away as if at horses and riders long lost in the dust.

A small radio near his pillow screeched endlessly. "It keeps me from thinkin'," he said.

It was still going when with colors flying, the greatest

jockey who ever rode a horse, dashed down the one way track forever.

He was hurried to an undertaking parlor. Large horse-shoes of flowers were piled around him. A florid minister whose duty it was to talk over all alike, said that the man who now lay before him still walked on the right hand of God the Father in Heaven.

He did not know how much Tod would have hated to walk, even had his companion been God. But the jockey was not aware. Words were now as nothing to one whose music had been the thundering hoofs of horses.

No room ever held such a gathering. Tears were in the eyes of rich and poor.

More than the minister were aware that the man they honored had walked with kings without losing the common touch.

But all was over and done for Tod.

The surpliced minister stopped talking. The tracks of the world were quiet.

PAUL BERN

PAUL BERN

A super-civilized man, he was an old world priest in a cathedral of terra cotta. Though he accepted and defended sham as the underlying ritual in the business that made up his life, he was, measured by his surroundings, a nobly great man.

One would need the power and patience of Stendahl to trace the many rivulets in his chaotic nature.

My close friend for years, he added the most ironical chapter to the turgid history of Hollywood. His love of glamour was blended with the philosophic humility of Spinoza.

Of medium height, small very brown eyes, a round body and face, Oriental in appearance, with the courtly manner of a mandarin, there was in him a lascivious torrent under suave control.

One of nineteen children, Paul Bern came from Prussia to New York at ten years of age. Learning a new language, he graduated from high school at sixteen and became a stenographer.

With that streak of the theatrical which coursed like a muddy river through the golden fields of his nature, he studied dramatic art. As an actor, he toured with a troup of players under Sarah Bernhardt. Though Sarah was ancient as the search for truth, the young player with the javelins of persecution in his make-up had his first complex concerning her. She was glamorous and personified wealth and he was very poor. With his admiration for the raucously divine termagant was a finer quality. Obtaining two tickets for each performance, he would watch the line in front of the theatre. When he found a couple who seemed more abjectly poor than the rest, he would present them with the tickets.

Rebuffed by Sarah, who was busy with lesser men, he turned to a rising young actress named Dorothy Millette. Dazzling as the morning sun, he was soon hopelessly infatuated with her.

His devotion followed her to a sanatorium. When he took her candy and flowers, and performed all the little courtesies with which his nature was so rich, she repaid him with abuse.

There followed a period of intense application to all things theatrical. He then "went into pictures" and became the master of false situations, the magician of shallow emotions at an enormous salary. His starved life took wings. Though he did not deviate from what he considered his duty to stand by the unfortunate girl, the brilliant neurotic started on the career of which poverty had denied him. All the gilded darlings of the films were potential Bernhardts.

Encouraging those who leaned, he quickly became a financial pillar. Though Hollywood poured its woes into his ears, the lattice of his confessional was not wide enough. Gentle and unctuous to all, he whiled away his leisure in the company of the taw drily glamorous, contending that only pain was real, a pagan and a hedonist, he wanted the sun, the ripple on the wave, the flash of beauty, youth and laughter. But he turned quickly from all of these at a tale of woe.

Ruled by his emotions, but deeply intelligent, he cared nothing for intelligence in Hollywood girls, but much for appearance. A beautiful girl might suffer in cheap attire, but he could not take her to dinner in public until she had an expensive fur coat.

This quality alone kept him from walking step by step with Christ.

His secretary's chief concern was to keep enough of his two thousand weekly salary in the bank to supply the demands upon him. If this failed, he would empty his pocket of the currency it contained.

A tattered old woman waited in his outer office. Unable to see her, he sent what money he had—and a note of apology.

"It's mine no more than hers," he said.

His father had been a saint, if one so defined can beget nineteen children in an economically disorganized world.

As a boy Paul had taken a stamp to mail a letter without asking his employer. Contrite, he told his gentle father. That patriarch wept over his crestfallen boy.

"My son," he said, "I would rather see you in your grave."

"A cheerful soul, Paul," I said.

"But you'd have loved him, Jim," he returned.

The father had once failed to give his nickel to a street car conductor. After leaving the car he became conscious of his crime and ran after it until he fell, exhausted. Returning home, he sent Paul with the coin to the headquarters of the company.

Paul's favorite word to all people in pain, and all were so to him, was "child".

"But I know, my dear child," he would say, even if the person were as old as human sorrow.

He became interested in a book I had. Called "The Great Abnormals", it concerned men of genius caught in conventional traps. He read it often and bought many copies for others.

He talked with concern of making biographical films of Schopenhauer, Nietzsche and Spinoza, then turned to producing "Susan Lennox" with Greta Garbo.

Touched by a high moment in a film, I asked him why it had failed commercially.

"Because the boy didn't get the girl," he returned dolefully.

Knowing German well, he acquired the great books of that language, and fondled them as if they were hurt children.

Though his heart was of vast dimensions, he could lock it now and then, and not explain why. One temporarily well known girl made demands by telephone, even while he conferred with his superior, Irving Thalberg. He would always hurry to her. He finally told his secretary he did not wish to receive her telephone calls. She then came to his office. He greeted her kindly, left his office and did not return until she had gone. He did not see her again.

He sent money without stint to another beautiful hoyden. Suddenly he stopped and never again looked at appeals from her.

Only once had he ever shown pique. He left a room when Bill Mizner continued to make slighting remarks about Jews. With Albert Lewin I went to him.

"Be a big boy, Paul. Mizner meant no harm," Lewin said.

"I'm so sorry, Al," returned Paul. "I couldn't help it—*they're my people.*"

He never again liked Mizner.

One of Irving Thalberg's lieutenants, he was very close to him. A man of great courage and temper, he was immovable before his acute chieftain.

When Albert Lewin joined Thalberg's staff, he found in Bern a man of kindly and deep consideration. Unusual in Hollywood, his ambition did not include stepping on the hands of another climber of the ladder.

Letters asking for help were always answered. He gave five thousand dollars in an effort to free Tom Mooney.

A DOZEN AND ONE

He sent for me on the day that Sacco and Vanzetti died. Arriving, I saw that his eyes were swollen.

"This will never do, Paul. You can't cry over all those who die in social wars."

His eyes went over me. "For shame, Jim. They belong to you now—your pity is only for the dead." Feeling he had hurt me, he said, "I'm so sorry—forgive me."

Years before, the ruler of a studio, he had discharged me. I had called him a practical idealist.

"We're even now," he said.

Having dedicated a book to him and Albert Lewin "for understanding", it was my turn to understand.

For a hundred years his forbears had been highly sensitized, erotic lovers of music, art and literature. Refined too much, he was the essence of the emotionally disembodied, and yet fiercely emotional. Above life, he was yet of it, as the cloud is of the rain.

Then he met Jean Harlow. Young and lovely as a kitten, and with no more thought, the beautiful blonde was different from other girls—for him. She first came to his office wearing a simple print dress and an innocent expression. That was enough. The dying embers burned again in the gentle masochist's heart. For the first time he began to worry about his marital status with the woman he had not seen for years. He came to me at the Panama Canal Zone. We talked long of the step he was taking. He wanted a home—"a flower in my garden". His three acres beyond Beverly Hills had been landscaped for years. His house, originally of exquisite taste, had been coated over by the varnish of Hollywood yokels at huge expense.

"Paul," I said, "why don't you coast to the end now instead of pursuing beautiful girls with million dollar bodies and ten cent heads?"

"Beauty is all there is," he returned.

He left, by plane, for Hollywood.

I went to Dorothy Millette, his common law wife. She had lived for many years in a New York hotel. I had brought her news of Paul in my frequent journeys to the city. When I now explained what Paul thought was a difficult situation, she reached the peak of human grandeur.

"Tell him he is always free," she said. "I will gladly step aside for so good and fine a man."

The result of my errand conveyed by telephone, Paul said, "A noble girl."

Before long, he married Jean Harlow. He was never again the same. His brilliant brain through which surged all the higher attributes, began to disintegrate. His compassion, a huge awning under which all could find shelter, now flapped in every wind. He was too morbid about hurt people in a world where hurting was the rule of life. His humor, never strong, withered away.

A DOZEN AND ONE

The sad honeymoon over, he came late to my house one night with a marked paragraph in a small leather volume of Conrad:

> "She was beautiful and had a weakness.
> We loved her no less for that. We
> admired her qualities aloud, we boasted
> of them to one another, as though
> they had been our own, and the
> consciousness of her only fault
> we kept buried in the silence of
> our profound affection."

I handed the book to him. There was so little to say—yet everything. I had not seen him drink before. He now took several brandies, and said, "Conrad's a great opium, when your heart's heavy, Jim. I like his—'Strength is nothing to boast of when you have it—it merely arises from the weakness of others'."

He put down the empty glass.

For years he had defended the morals of Hollywood women. He now trembled. The abstract might be an actuality.

"She's so lovely," he went on in the tone of a lost but still enraptured shepherd boy.

I would not even dispute an enemy who talked of a loved one.

"Don't you agree?" he asked.

"Yes, she's very lovely," I replied.

"Lovely, lovely," he repeated the word again, with deep sadness in his eyes.

Fond of powerful etchings, he had given me one of sheep perishing in the snow. Above was a wooden crucifix, while all around was the swirling white desolation. He looked at it for some time, then said, "They're wondering what it's all about. *So am I.*"

He opened the door. "So long, Jim," he said.

His powerful car turned in the direction of Beverly Hills.

Soon his suicide was in all the papers. Beside him was a letter to Jean Harlow. "Last night was only a comedy," he wrote.

He had undoubtedly been alone for hours. What his thoughts were, wandering about his dream nest, no man will ever know. The winds of life had been too strong for the vivid light in his brain.

Paul had left a void in passing. Many looked elsewhere for support.

As she was a valuable star, everything was done to protect Jean Harlow. She was then in the middle of a production.

His friends, in the business which he had exalted, allowed the gossip to go over the world that he had injured the lovely blonde. The truth was more simple.

There had been several suicides in his immediate family. He had reached the end.

A DOZEN AND ONE

Passing an ancient cripple, he had said, "My God—what does she want to live for?"

The gorgeous Harlow, so soon to die in the middle of another film, had been merely his furbelow with destiny —the last rose in his wind-blown garden.

My house was besieged by reporters. Could I identify a photograph of Dorothy Millette?

I knew she had been in Hollywood. She was expected soon again from Hawaii. No doubt seeing the dismal years ahead without her generous protector, she jumped from a boat in the Sacramento River.

An actor talked over all that was mortal of the brilliant Bern, while leaders of the film industry allowed their greatest man to be patronized.

"Paul was just a naive child," the actor said.

I did not agree. Paul was a thousand years old at birth. Into his soul had seeped the frustrations of generations forever silent. No more a child than Dean Swift, he was no more naive than Freud.

WALTER WINCHELL

WALTER WINCHELL

The highest paid gossip in the world, he can more readily keep a secret than any person in it. The most original man in America, an artist among journalists, a hornet with a soul, his column appears in nearly two thousand newspapers. In George Bernard Shaw's opinion Walter Winchell writes as though he had discovered the business.

In the U. S. Navy during the first World War and a member of the Naval Reserve since, he is now a lieutenant commander.

Learning early the patter of life from those who faced the economic bullets, he became their spokesman. As a result, he is certain of at least a footnote in the history of these times.

With a part time job, collecting news for a theatrical weekly, he left school at thirteen to go on the stage with Gus Edwards' NEWSBOYS SEXTETTE. In that way he could get more news.

George Jessel, one of the group, now a famous entertainer, says, "Walter was always busy collecting news between shows."

To those who believe that character does not change, Jessel's words are significant.

At seventeen Winchell toured the country in his own vaudeville sketch. He then returned to Broadway, and began his newspaper career. His struggle was not easy; but of that, nothing from Winchell.

A DOZEN AND ONE

A period followed when he operated his own tabloid, getting news, then editing and publishing it.

Not hearing the clock that chimed his luckiest hour, he went for a "scoop". A young woman dancer was said to have adopted a baby. Winchell knocked at her door early in the morning and explained that he had come for the story.

"Ask the baby," the young woman said, "but don't wake it."

He learned later that she had not adopted the child. "I lost the story but won the girl." His marriage to June Magee is one of the happiest on record.

With the poise of the Irish, she is the keystone of his turbulent career. The orchids he so flamboyantly hands out are generally of her selection. Her natural tendency is for the under dog—"But so is Walter's," she stated.

His name became a household word when Hearst signed him. As confident in his own star as if he had placed it in the sky, he has been near the hopes and fears of people for nearly twenty years.

The current crystalizer of thought, he has coined many words and phrases—those divorced in Reno are *Renovated*. Of one fellow: he has a charming way of never amounting to anything. Of another: he always leaves you with a nice taste in your heart. Of still another: the nicest thing about him is that he's nice to people he doesn't have to be nice to. Of a lady trouble maker: she's in more jams than strawberries. Of a girl's beauty: she looks better on the telephone.

Seeing a woe-begone youngster near the Lambs' Club, he called him "Somebody's bundle from Heaven". The phrase appeared in his column and touched the heart of America.

Nothing escapes him. "Things are so confused in Washington that even German spies don't know what's going on."

I first met him at a dinner given by George Jean Nathan in honor of St. John Ervine, a visiting English dramatic critic and author of that excellent play "John Ferguson". Winchell was debonair and alert—Broadway when the sun is shining.

"Were you always a journalist?" the dramatist asked.

"No—I was a hoofer." Winchell looked at me. "So was this fellow—on the railroads."

St. John Ervine smiled. He had called me the loudest of the "God damn" school in American writing.

Winchell's mind was everywhere.

"I don't know how the devil he gets so much news— he never listens," Nathan said.

While he tried to explain the miracle of America to St. John Ervine, I asked Nathan why a certain politician took himself so seriously.

"Because," was the instant reply, "he hasn't yet learned the humor of being beaten."

Winchell turned from the Anglo-Irishman, and wrote the remark down. "I can't let a crack like that go."

The remark led his column.

"And I claimed he never listened," said Nathan.

He has no petty rancours. A rough and brash fighter, he will shake hands when the verbal battle is all over. His squabble with Westbrook Pegler is well known. "Westbrook's all right," he says of the master of acrimony and courage, "even if we don't agree."

When Al Jolson, offended at something he had said, aimed a blow at him, he ducked. "He came so close, I could smell his manicure," Winchell said. Never once did he use his column as a platform of vengeance.

A bellboy admirer said, "It's easier to read his stuff than wait on him."

"Why?"

"Because he's so cockeyed nervous. You're no sooner gone than he wants you back."

He is fond of his wife and children.

"I like my job—it gives me a lot of time with them."

There are two children in the Winchell clan—Walda, a young lady, and a boy, Walter, Jr.

Before the boy was born, Mrs. Winchell suggested that if it was a boy they call it Reed Winchell. Walter suggested that if it was a girl, the name of Sue Winchell would be quite approprite. Ben Bernie, hearing of the coming child, suggested over the radio that Lynch Winchell would be appropriate whether it was a boy or a girl.

"One up for Bernie," said Walter.

When Gloria, another daughter, died, her loss was borne by the parents with simple dignity.

When I mentioned Sam Butler having said "that sincerity was a youthful virtue," Walter smiled.

A boy was facing the electric chair in Oklahoma. His first letter to me opened with the words," I was a road kid like you and now I'm condemned to die."

I asked Walter to help me save the lad. "He's a poor kid who got in the game at dark and struck out."

"That's sad," said Walter.

"Yes—I feel something should be done for him."

"What, for instance?" he asked.

"I'd like your column for a pulpit," I said.

Walter studied. "You can have it—Jim, even if sincerity is a youthful virtue." He took my arm.

The boy's sentence was commuted to *life*.

At a dinner given later in Winchell's honor, scores of newspapermen assembled. Two after dinner speakers, both members of the "I knew him when" club, attended.

One raked Winchell's past over the coals. "He's made a couple of million peeking in keyholes."

The other gentleman praised him highly. "There was no place for him in newspaper work—so he made one."

The dinner over, Winchell came to me.

"That first fellow was hard on you, Walter."

"Oh, well—he had to say something. I threw the first rock." Winchell stopped a second. "I wanted to say something about the boy in Oklahoma, but those guys talked too long."

It was the Winchell I liked. Even with many things on his mind, he could think of a lad unknown to him who had escaped the electric chair.

Winchell became an ace reporter in the Lindbergh kidnapping case, by putting feeling into his work. A family man, he had no sympathy for one who would kidnap a child. He has been charged with going overboard in that case; of going beyond his business of reporting what happened. Winchell thought not of putting individuality above journalism. He has since greeted the mention of Lindbergh's name with silence. Even when George M. Cohan, of whom he was fond, asked, "What can you do with a guy who gets into a wheelbarrow and pushes himself across the Atlantic?" he was quiet.

It was that touch of nature between the aviator and himself—Lindbergh had lost a child; so had Winchell.

There was a detail at Hauptman's trial in the Lindbergh case as to whether or not a step-ladder could be put into an automobile. Riding down Fifth Avenue with Walter after going about New York with him, we stopped for a traffic light. Ahead of us was an automobile with a step-ladder inside.

WALTER WINCHELL

"There, there," pointed Walter.

Walter sleeps until mid-afternoon, then makes his rounds until early morning.

His headquarters is the teeming city instead of a certain night club. All talk to him. Catching the heart beats of the people, he hears more stories in a night than O. Henry could invent in a month. He writes and fits them into his pattern with more realism. His appearance at any place is magic. News happens around him. Habit makes him stop at certain places.

"If I could only get Winchell to mention my joint like he does a few others, I'd be rich," one tavern keeper said. "A mention by him is dynamite."

The keeper of the tavern was right.

He created great interest in Frank Scully's *Fun in Bed,* by saying, "It is a hundred times funnier than Ben Bernie's jokes and three hundred times funnier than mine."

Walter has long admired Scully. "The guy's been in hospitals most of his life—but never for his heart."

"Write to me from the south of France," he said to Scully. "I like to get letters from far places."

After reaching New York and having dinner with the owner of a night club, I walked from his gorgeous apartment to his place of business and was refused admittance because I had no necktie.

A DOZEN AND ONE

"I just came from the owner's house," I explained. "I was all right up there."

The man at the door was quizzical. "Orders is orders," he said.

He then offered me a necktie that not even a literary critic would wear.

"Was Winchell with you?" Alfred Strelsin asked.

"No," I replied. "Hitler could get in that joint—with Winchell."

Never intoxicated, Winchell is abstemious with food.

He was a favorite with Wilson Mizner. When the huge playboy told of Clarence Darrow saying, "I don't believe in murder but I've read many an obituary with pleasure," Walter laughed.

He bubbles with enthusiasm. The thing he is doing is the most important in the world—at the moment.

That which made Broadway known fifty years ago is "old news" to him.

The urchin with no respect for names, he twists them for a smile. Oscar Odd McIntyre, the famous columnist, was "the very odd McIntyre." St. John Ervine, verbose in his dramatic reviews, was "St. Yawn Ervine".

He told how a critic solved the problem of catching up on his sleep by attending the theatre. When another reviewer volunteered to tell him what the play was about he held up his hand, "Don't tell me—I want to write about it."

WALTER WINCHELL

The founder of the telegraphic style of writing a column, Winchell now has many able disciples: Leonard Lyons, Herb Caen, Sydney Skolsky and Louis Sobol, among them.

Strong for the right, he knows the furbelows of environment that make people wrong.

"There goes Walter Winchell," said a waiter. "He saved my life."

"How's that?" I asked.

"Well, as you know, I came up the hard way on the east side and all I remember is what I'd like to forget. I was workin' in a joint at eighteen per when Mosey— I knew from a kid, came in and asked me why I didn't go with him. He was makin' half a million bucks a year. It looked kinda good to me—so I mentioned it to Walter.

" 'Don't do it,' he says. 'Your record's clean, and you can sleep at night. The cops always let you alone. Besides, it's better to be in the rain alive, than dead under a roof,' he says.

"Mosey was shot the next week. I'll never forget Walter's crack about the rain."

As verses appearing in his column indicate, he is fond of all children:

"He's yours now and since I cannot have him back,
    I want to tell you certain things to do,
He likes his door left open—just a crack—
    (The dark can scare a little guy of two).

A DOZEN AND ONE

Put Mother Goose upon the nearest shelf,
  And keep a shabby 'Teddy' ever near.
And when you hear him laughing to himself
  Call all the angels in—so they can hear.

Be good to him and give him all the things
  That I can never give him any more . .
A puppy dog, a plane with silver wings,
  A Noah's Ark to sail the nursery floor.

And, Mary, when small angels go to bed,
Lean down for me—and kiss his curly head."

Each column is balanced by the keen eclectic, who learned how to select from life instead of college.

Daily the incessant flow of badinage continues: "the Japs now have a fleetless Tuesday . . . . If you think her curves are something, you ought to see her detours."

His New York apartment is known to but few. His large estate, an hour's drive from New York, has around it a high fence with a locked gate. His intimate friends do not tell each other where it is. "If Walter wants you to know, he'll tell you."

He is never quite at home in the country. His eyes often drift toward the city. For him the roses grow and fade on the streets of New York. The buzz of voices— "There's Walter Winchell"—is part of his life.

He is unapproached on the radio.

WALTER WINCHELL

The Frenchman who said it was no small thing to have a style of one's own, must have had him in mind.

He means his famous flash—"My job's to give the news." He takes his work seriously.

At the close of a radio broadcast in which his tenth year with the same sponsor was celebrated, a news item was handed to him. Dated Moscow, it read:

The Berlin radio reports that Adolf Hitler has been killed while inspecting Eastern Front defenses.

He read it quickly.

"Damn the luck," he screamed. "Hitler's dead and I'm off the air."

He became very still.

When told it was all a hoax, that Hitler was still alive, "Gee," he said, "I'd go off the air forever if no more bombs were dropped on babies, if no more people were shot because they believed in something different, if there would be no more prejudice with a gun in its hand."

He rubbed his forehead.

The jokers looked at one another.

"Come on, Walter," one said.

With head down, he left the building.

Soon the world was born again, as he made the rounds of New York.

HENRY ARMSTRONG

HENRY ARMSTRONG

Langston Hughes told me of a young Negro who wanted to write. I might be able to give him some pointers. "He's Henry Armstrong's trainer," he said.

He came with the poet. His name was Harry Armstrong. After a half hour Langston asked if he might bring Henry in. He had been the chauffeur for the others.

Henry was rated the third best featherweight in the world, having held the champion Freddy Miller even. He could get no work.

When he entered the room I knew at once there was a man in the house.

Well dressed and polite, he had the springy step of one with boundless energy. His shoulders were wide; his waist slender. His head was large and his eyes narrow. So tightly drawn was the skin across his leather pounded face, it might have been part of a bronze statue.

I liked him at once. With tigerish suppleness under control, he was the unspoiled primitive—on whom civilization rested lightly.

Forgetting literature for life, I shifted my interest to the groping bruiser.

When dinner was served, I had him seated across from me. I wanted his eyes—to face him as I might in an opposite corner. His interest was in the food. He ate while his trainer talked.

One of fourteen children, he was born "the baby of

the family" in St. Louis. Like Joe Louis and Jack Dempsey he was part Cherokee Indian.

His trainer had been in college. He had fought for six years—"just another palooka". Discouraged, he met Henry. The lad wanted to enter the ring. Harry put the gloves on with him "just for pastime". Before it was over he saw in the young aspirant a future great fighter. He trained him for a year, then changed his name from Jackson to Armstrong.

As mixed matches were not allowed in Missouri, he took Henry to Pittsburgh in an old car. "We got a couple of fights but no money." They arrived back in St. Louis before the car collapsed.

Henry went to work driving spikes on a railroad twelve miles from home. The hours were long; the work hard. With no money for carfare he walked, trotted, and ran to labor. Once there, he swung a sledge. These things made his legs and shoulders the most powerful of any man his weight in the world.

He fought a few times in the ring. The contests threw no light on his then dark future. Discouraged, his young manager induced him to beat his way to California.

Being Negroes, they had a hard time on the road.

"We did a little panhandling," said Harry. "We'd work for food or money if we could get it."

There was little work and less food.

After two weeks the dark young rovers reached Los

HENRY ARMSTRONG

Angeles, hungry and tired. For several days they lived on fruit stolen from a stand. "Henry stole one bunch of grapes, but he put it back. But he ate what I stole. He wasn't too scrupulous to do that," said the trainer.

The pugilist looked at me. We both smiled. Harry had emphasized the word scrupulous.

They made no headway in Los Angeles. Leroy Haynes, another dark bruiser, took them to Thomas Cox, who was connected with "bootleg amateur clubs". Mr. Cox secured several engagements for Henry at three dollars an engagement.

"Henry hurt his shoulder in the third fight," said his trainer.

The fighter continued to eat.

Mr. Cox, not being in the business of financing wandering bruisers, suggested that Harry fight. And Harry did. "I had to have money to take care of Henry." Fearful of going slug nutty and realizing he could never be a great fighter, the indomitable lad went to the leather wars.

When Henry's shoulder healed, they talked things over with Mr. Cox. That gentleman thought of another gentleman. "Wirt Ross is a big shot," he said. "He might get Henry over."

Mr. Ross paid Mr. Cox $250.00 for Henry, who was a minor. The papers were sent to St. Louis to be signed by his father.

"That was when our hardships really began," the trainer remembered. "Ross told a lot of funny jokes, but he didn't get Henry many fights."

Henry smiled. His plate was empty.

He slashed his way through the preliminaries, until he got $250.00 for main bouts. "By the time Ross took his cut and the money he'd advanced Henry and me—well, we were soon broke again."

Good news came. Henry was booked to fight four hundred miles away for $300.00. They went to the fight in the manager's small roadster. Mr. Ross was a large man. Henry occupied what was left of the seat. "I sat in the rumble," said Harry. While the fighter was intent on other food, his trainer continued dolefully, "It never failed to rain. By the time we got home, Ross had all the money and we had all the worry."

Henry again smiled.

As a build-up—the mortar for the career of another man—Henry was offered $1500.00 to *lose* to Arizmendi in Mexico City. Though that was a lot of money, "Henry forgot to lose."

In spite of such a lack of memory, Arizmendi, badly beaten, was given the decision.

The contest created such great interest that Henry was offered $2500.00 to *lose* a return bout. He again left California for Mexico to face Arizmendi.

The fight was highly publicized.

"Tell that nigger of yours he's got to lose a lot surer this time," Arizmendi's manager said to Ross.

"Okeh," said Ross.

"I've got to have his trainer's word," the Mexican's manager insisted. "He has influence with his fighter."

"He'll sure lose again," assured Harry.

The manager of the Mexican, still wary, said, "I know where you can get a $2000.00 bet on Arizmendi."

"I wish I was a bettin' man—for Henry'll sure lose," said Harry. "Besides, I haven't got the money."

"I'll loan you two thousand," the manager offered.

The trainer took the money. "I had to make it look good."

The fight was held in the bull ring. Mexico City swarmed with people. Forty thousand saw the battle.

Harry did not mention the two thousand he had bet on the other side. "I didn't want no hobble on a good horse like Henry."

The fighter was busy with his ice cream.

"We never saw such a crowd," said the trainer. "You remember, Henry?"

"That's right," was the answer. The ice cream vanished.

"Anyhow, they picked Arizmendi up from the floor and raised his hand," said Henry.

But they did not see the money. Mr. Ross had trusted the promoters. They decamped, so he explained.

A DOZEN AND ONE

Mr. Ross had never been so careless before. But that was water down the mountain.

Money was needed at once. The trainer thought of the money he had bet. How could he collect it? Meeting young Joe Rivers, a favorite fighter in Mexico City, he told him his plight.

"It'll look funny if I collect it," Harry said. "Like we'd sold out."

"I'll get you the money—you won it," the fighter said.

"I just had to tell Henry. He never said a word—after all we were busted."

Henry reached for his coffee.

There were no further fights in Mexico City. "Henry was just too dangerous. He couldn't learn how to pull a punch," explained Harry. "He was in the ring to fight. But that was no matter—that boy Rivers was a good friend. He got me what I'd won but didn't mean to— and Henry just took it like it was a purse. We both like Rivers a lot—he was mighty decent. He stayed with us till we left."

They thought of many things on the long journey to California. "We're getting no place fast," I said to Henry.

"I know," was all Henry said.

A deep silence followed.

The three dark young men were intense.

"You might see a way out, Jim," Langston Hughes

said. "Henry and Harry here are two mighty fine boys."

Henry's eyes were directly on me.

"You've come up the hard way," I said, "you've learned the rules by getting in there and slugging. You can lick any man within twenty pounds of your weight in the world. You don't have to bargain because you're dark. Joe Louis hasn't. There are a lot of decent people who follow fights."

"That's what we've decided," said the trainer. "From now on it's kill or be killed."

"What have you on for the future, Henry?" I asked him.

"Arizmendi—the Olympic—here in Los—two weeks," was the answer.

Having traded blows for bread, I knew that Henry was not a "mouth fighter".

"Henry's beaten him twice and lost two decisions—he's innocent and honest, and it isn't right," Langston Hughes put in.

"But you'll beat him again, I said to the fighter.

Henry's head went up and down.

A thought came to me.

"Will Ross sell his contract?" I asked the trainer.

"Sure thing," replied Harry.

"How much?"

"Three thousand, maybe," was the answer.

It would not be too much of a gamble. If I knew

pugilists, and I felt I did, the bronze boy before me was a world beater. The cards had fallen the wrong way— otherwise he would have been the champion. The ring still lured me. I could be a writer any time. It was life I needed.

Ego helped me to recall when I was a bruiser with a whalebone body and a granite jaw. If nothing else, those days had brought me understanding and admiration for the floundering fighter before me. That was something.

"I'd like to fight for you, Mr. Tully," the bronze bruiser said.

"Maybe you will, Henry," I returned.

We left the table.

"Well, Harry, we haven't talked much about writing," I said.

"It's the stuff that makes writing," said Langston Hughes.

Henry closed one hand and struck his open palm. Closing the other he reversed the procedure. His muscles writhed beneath his well fitting coat as he did so.

"You'll hear from me," I said as poet, fighter and trainer left.

For days the idea burned in my head. I would again enter the wild world of the bruiser. The thought made the bubbles burst in my blood. It would be a return to the care-free days I'd loved I had fought hard for freedom and found it another jail.

HENRY ARMSTRONG

I had made my contribution—had written with honesty and conviction about the people from whom I came.

I went to see Henry fight Arizmendi. He was no longer the meek boy, but a ripping, slashing, tearing fighter. Arizmendi was no set-up. The Negro's blows, hard and accurate as five pound sledges, were everywhere. So was Arizmendi.

Once again I was in the noisy and whirring harbour of forgetfulness.

Both men stood in the center of the ring at the beginning of the tenth and final round. Neither had a decided edge. Either could be given the fight.

The Mexican quarter sent up wild cheers for Arizmendi.

The heads of the fighters crashed. They grunted from the force of the blows.

A crashing right from the Mexican. Henry went to one knee. The blow sent the wild horses dashing.

Shrapnel cracking against a wall. The murderous Henry charged. Arizmendi stood solid under the fusilade of leather. Henry's trainer had forgotten his ambition to write.

"Harder, Henry boy," he shouted.

There was a minute to go.

Henry's blows came harder. Not one, but a hundred, they crashed in an avalanche of fury. The brave Mexican lashed back. His blows had no effect on the whirling dark tide. He went back for a second. His relentless antagonist moved in.

"Harder, Henry, harder," the would-be writer screamed.

The dark arms, now swelling ramrods, moved with terrible precision.

The blows threw Arizmendi against the ropes. He caught Armstrong with a left and right. The Negro staggered back—Arizmendi began to move from the rope. The Negro pinned him with blows.

"Harder, Henry, harder," yelled Harry.

Screams from the audience came with the fury of the blows that followed. There was no escape from the driving leather.

Arizmendi sagged, then covered.

The bell rang.

Armstrong's hand was raised in victory.

Scenes at the ringside became tortures in my mind. Not the fight, but the surroundings were remembered.

The dream at last collided with reality. Sadly and reluctantly I turned to the austere and lonely business that made up my life.

"I can't make it, Henry," I said to the great young bruiser.

"I'm sorry," he said. "I just know we could go places together."

"So do I, Henry," I returned. "But the game would take too much of my time."

He nodded. "I know. She is a tough racket."

Henry trainer then asked my opinion of Al Jolson. "He said he'd buy the contract if Eddie Mead'd manage him."

"Mead and Jolson are both right people," I said. "None better."

The comedian bought the contract for ten thousand dollars.

Henry's first fight under the new set-up was with Joe Rivers, who had been such a friend in Mexico. Rivers was in bad luck. There was sickness in his home. If he stayed the limit with Henry, it would mean another fight with bigger money.

Always grateful for kindness, the boys faced a definite problem. Rumors had spread that Rivers was to stay.

The trainer came to me. "You said it, Harry," I told him. "It's kill or be killed."

"I know," said the trainer, "but it's a shame we've got to fight Rivers—he was a swell friend."

"Maybe so," I returned, "but he'll knock Henry out if he can and feel sorry later."

It was all a muddle. Here were lads too innately decent for the rough careers they followed.

"Come, Harry," I said to the boy who was as much a poet as Langston Hughes.

We devised a plan.

He went to the fighter. "You know, Henry," he said, "Mr. Tully and Mr. Jolson have each bet a thousand dollars on you winning by a knockout."

That was enough for the great fighter. He went to Rivers' dressing room. "Do your best, Joe," he said. "If you knock me out, it's okeh—and no hard feelings if I do the same with you."

"Okeh, Hank," returned his opponent.

It was a desperate battle until the dark bruiser began to get the range. He then rattled blows swift as machine gun fire.

Rivers went down. His muscles jerked a few times. Armstrong watched anxiously until the count was finished. He then helped his defeated benefactor to his corner.

"I just hated to but I couldn't do nothin' else," he said.

A record never equaled, he won twenty-six fights by knockouts the next year.

In the year that followed he won three titles—the featherweight at 128 pounds from Pete Sarron, the lightweight at 133 pounds from Lou Ambers and the welterweight at 142 pounds from that division's great champion, Barney Ross. This record has not been remotely approached.

Jack Johnson called him the greatest fighter in thirty years.

"One of the greatest fighters ever," said Dempsey.

He came to my house once again. The same gentle lad, success had thrown his shoulders back.

His trainer, Harry, accompanied him. He did not discuss his ambition to write.

While the trainer talked of the many ring encounters of his fighter, that debonair fellow buried himself, chuckling, in the cartoons of "Esquire".

We gazed at him. "He's a very great yarn, Harry," I said. "You ought to write it."

With the knowledge of writing that cannot be taught, he said, "I'm a little too close."

The fighter closed the magazine. I walked with him under the trees.

"Henry," I said, "you've gone to the leather wars at least a dozen times since we met. What do you think of all the lads you've beaten?"

He did not answer right away. Instead, his eyes followed a raucous red-headed woodpecker.

"I really don't know, Mr. Tully—they're just too game."

Lou Ambers had been given the lightweight championship in a return bout. A draw would have been the only fair verdict. Low punches had cost Armstrong the decision.

"What do you think of Ambers, Henry?"

"He's a mighty nice boy and a good fighter," was the answer.

No longer the driver of a cheap car for a poet and a youth who wanted to write, the well tailored conqueror of three champions seated himself behind the wheel of a vivid powerful roadster.

"So long, Mr. Tully," he said, "I won't be soon forgettin' you."

"That goes for both of us," said his trainer.

Long after they had gone, I thought of the barbed wire entanglements of life and for an instant regretted not buying the contract.

The ropes of the ring of memory moved.

H. L. MENCKEN

H. L. MENCKEN

In the vernacular of the ring he would be known as Baby Face Mencken. Life has written no line upon his face. Round and innocent, there is no indication of the powerful brain behind it. His eyes are so wide open they seem to arch his forehead. They are the windows to the Mencken mansion. Alert and all seeing, they have pity, sentimentality and ribald laughter.

He has too many ideas he wants to express to be an attentive listener. Words fall like drops of water concerning pugilists and thieves, biology and dreams, politics and prisons.

His left foot turns in as he walks. His stride is swift as his mind. His head is big and round. His ears protrude. His teeth are large, white and irregular. His shoulders are broad and slightly rounded. He bathes in cold water and trims his fingernails with a jack knife. Careless of posture, he is always well tailored.

Behind his bland smile is a charming curiosity. He wears his learning so casually it may easily be overlooked in the burning vigor of the man. The universe enthralls him. Everything has his attention.

Scornful of democracy, he considers the automobile a nuisance, and rides the street cars, fraternizing with all those caught up in the mad disquiet of living. Everything matters to him; the turn of a phrase, the cadence of music, the pronunciation or derivation of a word or the crying of a little child. His passion is for honest work.

His integrity is vast—his penetration deep. His comrades for years have never known him to do a small thing.

Of German, Scotch and English descent, Henry Louis Mencken was born the first of four children, in Baltimore, in 1880.

When he was three his father moved the family to 1524 Hollins Street. With but a short interlude, the dynamic iconoclast has lived there since. Of brick, trimmed in white marble, it is three stories high and directly upon the street. He works on the third floor alone, oblivious of all.

His father died in 1899—his mother in 1926. For over forty years she went daily to market, a basket on her arm. The family life was ideal. Neither quarrel nor misunderstanding ever took place in the home.

Mencken studied engineering as a youth. He graduated from Polytechnic at the age of sixteen, in 1896. His father offered him one hundred dollars if he carried off highest honors. He won the money by breaking all existing school records with an average of ninety-six. He delivered the honorary address at the commencement and has hated oratory since.

As a boy he read "the whole of Thackeray in one winter and then proceeded backward to Addison, Steele, Pope, Swift, Jonson, and the other magnificos of the eighteenth century." He also read Shakespeare, Keats, Shelley, Byron and Herrick in his teens.

H. L. MENCKEN

He became a helper in his father's cigar factory and did not attend college.

Securing a job as an "extra reporter", he worked six days a week at the factory and seven evenings on the newspaper. He was next given a regular job as a reporter at eight dollars a week, and soon after a raise when about to go to a rival newspaper. Within a year he was earning eighteen dollars a week.

Each Sunday morning he "covered" the cathedral then presided over by Cardinal Gibbons. As the aging prelate delivered about the same sermon each Sunday, Mencken remained away one Sunday and inserted the usual item in the paper. Aroused that Sunday, the Cardinal delivered a sermon that made the front page. The young reporter was chagrined "and so was the editor".

He was city editor at nineteen. At twenty he wrote the souvenir book for the new Baltimore court house and comic stanzas for Lew Dockstader, and newspaper features for syndicates.

He next tried to write a novel in which Shakespeare was the principal character. Unable to manipulate Shakespeare in a book, he decided to see the world by taking a ship for the Bahamas. He missed the boat, and shipped on a British vessel bound for Jamaica. Deserting with the captain's knowledge, he loitered for some time.

Then a job opened on a Baltimore newspaper. With his usual energy and capacity, he became managing editor at twenty-four, and editor-in-chief at twenty-five. He also ran a literary and dramatic column "on the side". With a sense of diabolic fairness, he had space reserved for those who wished to answer any charges he made.

His first published work was "Ventures into Verse". It was not a happy venture. On the title page was "First (and last) edition".

When the Baltimore Herald suspended publication, he was offered work on the New York Times. His love of home, blending with his dislike of New York, made him refuse.

Before taking up active work again he wrote his book on Nietzsche. One of the finest studies of the brilliant madman ever written, the author was twenty-eight when the book appeared. The cantankerous German made an indelible impression upon him. Like Nietzsche, he has little intellectual sympathy for those who become stragglers in the forced economic march of the present.

Mencken next became co-editor of the "Smart Set" with George Jean Nathan at a salary of fifty dollars a week.

Though he has spent more time reading the manuscripts of unsuccessful writers than any other editor in America, his dictum is "a bad writer has no rights whatever. Any mercy shown him is wasted and mistaken."

A young laborer once sent him a story. Mencken replied, "You write so well that an idea occurs to me. Why not try something for 'The American Mercury'?" The laborer was exalted. Within a month Mencken received an article from him. He read it diligently and returned it with painstaking corrections. After the laborer had re-writen it Mencken accepted the manuscript. In three years James Stevens became nationally known as the author of "Paul Bunyan", "Brawnyman" and "Mattock".

Mencken developed a convict writer in the same way. His first letter of rejection read, "This story belongs to a type that I dislike. Why don't you write about real people—that is, people you have actually known? They are much more interesting. I suggest an article on life in prison, a picture of the week's round. What is amusing there? What do you find in men? What I have in mind is an article wholly avoiding the question of the utility of prisons. Accept the thing as it stands, and describe it. What do prisoners laugh at? What do they talk of? Is there any social rank? Is there politics?"

Months passed and with them were many rejections for the convict. Each rejection had a letter with it. At last a leter reached the convict—"Thanks very much for "The First Day". It is excellent stuff, and I am putting it into type at once. A check and proof will reach you in about a week." The author, Robert Tasker, is now a successful scenarist.

There are many writers, painters, scientists, sculptors and musicians who owe much to his encouragement.

A DOZEN AND ONE

Accused by literary adversaries of having no knowledge of books written since 1880, he has encouraged and understood the leading writers of his generation.

Not considered an emotional man, his feeling for emotion in literature is deep. His praise of Willa Cather's "My Antonia" brought a larger audience for that fine novel.

As an editor, he seldom held a manuscript over three days. His reasons for refusal or acceptance were succinct. Payment was prompt. "A writer wants his money; he may even take a little less to get it right away."

Often, if he thought an article or story might find a place in a magazine with a greater circulation and more revenue than "The American Mercury", he would explain to the writer and offer to withdraw.

After long effort I gained admission to the last issue of "Smart Set". Over a year passed and my second book, "Beggars of Life", appeared. He reviewed the book and asked if I had any more vagabond incidents such as it contained. I contributed many to "The American Mercury".

He has more detachment than his writing indicates. When a Communist berated him as "the bum of Baltimore" because I, as his protégé, had written a book that was not all, in his opinion, it should have been, Mencken encouraged the attacker until he had also written a book.

Mencken's capacity for work is enormous. Leaving a

sixty thousand word manuscript with him when we parted at three in the morning, he telephoned me before twelve. He had taken fifteen thousand words from the story for his "American Mercury".

During another period I brought him a nine thousand word manuscript and asked for a decision before dinner. He read for twenty minutes while I chatted with Mrs. Mencken. He then removed his horn rimmed glasses and said, "It's in, Jim. You've nailed the yeggs to the wall."

His hidden pity is for the living artists; men and women caught in the snares of huge social forces. It is vast for the reason that it takes in the incomprehensible.

I covered an execution for him and called it "A California Holiday". He opened the files of his magazine to include it in an anniversary number. Months later at a table in Baltimore, he talked of the hanged man's fate and of the whirligigs in his destiny.

He is not always serious on questions pertaining to the race. At breakfast with Judge Ben B. Lindsey, we listened while the judge poured out his ideas in behalf of birth control.

"It will never do," said Mencken. "We must have a future generation to run the gasoline stations."

He was interested in Lindsey as a man of courage and character.

An evangelist of beauty, he will explain Keats to a longshoreman. His politeness springs from deep feeling.

A DOZEN AND ONE

A helpless old man makes him forget Nietzsche.

In spite of having written that "Love is the delusion that one woman differs from another," he was married in middle life to Sara Haardt, a sensitive and beautiful girl with ability as a creative writer. He made happy and congenial the last ten years of her life. She died at thirty-seven.

I recall a picture of him bringing the paraphernalia of a fireplace to her on a Sunday morning. The worshippers in the cathedral nearby were disturbed as a hundred and ninety pound man and a taxi driver wrestled with iron and brass.

A caricaturist with the sensibilities of a great artist, he likes a tale with a lash at the end. When told of a crusader's plight he listened attentively. Captured by a group of men who were opposed to his theories of social justice, they stripped him to the waist and begun to burn the letters I.W.W. on him with the ends of hot cigars.

"I'm not an I.W.W.," he shouted.

"Then what are you?" asked the leader.

"An I.W.W. *sympathizer*," was the answer.

"All right then, we'll burn that on."

Mencken's laughter was loud and long.

With the same horror of liberty for the herd that he has for a stupid king, or insincere president, he is continually in mental hot water. With his cronies over a bottle or vat of wine or beer, he becomes as forgetful of human grief as a gambler of the hunger of another day.

With the expansiveness of the politician in public, he is termed a "good mixer". Many are fond of him. His power over others is simple humanity. Though capable of affection, few reach the inner hall of his friendship. Not liking to be moved deeply, wsen the winds of emotion howl he takes refuge in the forest of the cynic.

His place as a literary critic I will leave to more pretentious men.

Such lines as the following which he wrote on Beethoven will never be surpassed—

"One hears harsh roars of cosmic laughter, vast splutterings of transcendental mirth, echoing and re-echoing down the black corridors of empty space. . . .

"His most complicated structures retained the overwhelming clarity of the Parthenon. . . .

"What lifted Beethoven above Haydn above all other men of music, save perhaps Bach and Brahms, was simply his greater dignity as a man. The feelings that Haydn put into tone were the feelings of a country pastor, a rather civilized stock broker. When he wept it was with the tears of a woman who has discovered another wrinkle; when he rejoiced it was with the joy of a child on Christmas morning. But the feelings that Beethoven put into his music were the feelings of a god. There was something Olympian in his snarls and rages, and there was a touch of hell fire in his mirth. He concerns himself not with the puerile agonies of love, but with the eternal tragedy of man. He is a great tragic poet, and like all great tragic poets, he is obsessed by a sense of the inscrutable meaninglessness of life."

Above the confusion of those who bring old comparisons to new and vital men, he said of a tale by Conrad, "As it stands it is austerely and beautifully perfect, just as the slow movement of the Unfinished Symphony is perfect."

He talks as he writes, in terms of music.

He is big enough to reprimand himself for overlooking an important phase of a story. "Certainly I thought I knew 'The End of the Tether' as well as I know anything in this world—and yet there was that incredible misunderstanding of it lodged firmly in my mind."

He dismissed H. G. Wells in a few pages, giving him a high place a few times as artist, and the rest—a sociological popinjay.

With a group of other newspaper men, he held a pseudo lynching for the edification of an English novelist. When the fearful stage was set, the leader of the mob asked the seemingly scared Ethiopian if he knew the nature of the love life.

"No suh," was the answer, "that's why they's hangin' me."

He is one of the oldest members of a club in Baltimore. Organized about forty years ago, it meets each Saturday night at the home of a different member. The women of the house load a table with food and liquids. At eight the women disappear; the banquet begins. Beer flows and ideas rise. At ten the table is partly cleared. The music begins. There is only one rule. If you are critical of the music you are thrown out. Coats are removed. Each member fondles his instrument of noisy torture.

There are many divergent opinions regarding Mencken.

According to Frank Harris, "He is kindly as only the honest can afford to be."

His co-worker, George Jean Nathan, says, "He is the defender of all who would make a path for the truth. He is above the malice and envy of little men. In the realm of ideas he has supreme detachment."

A parlor socialist wrote that his prose had the sound of large stones being thrown into a dump cart.

A professor of academic English asserted that his sentences moved forward with the violence of a Wagner overture and the formlessness of jazz.

A minister of the gospel stated that he lacked the essential qualifications of the role he essayed, and could deal only in boorish vituperation, with a vocabulary borrowed from Billingsgate and the Bowery.

An editor claimed that his style affected one like the din of interminable riveting.

In O. O. McIntyre's opinion he was a Baltimore Babbitt.

A DOZEN AND ONE

To a gentleman of Mississippi he was the buzzard of American literature—a wild eyed, loud mouthed, jackass.

To John Farrar, his creed was anti-American because he did not understand the poetry of America.

A professor considered any woman who cooked a good meal his superior in intelligence.

A writer in Los Angeles called him an 18-carat, 23-jewel, 33rd degree, bred in the bone and dyed in the wool moron.

To J. B. Priestly, the English writer, he is a roaring and bellowing Democrat.

Billy Sunday, the evangelist, exclaimed, "Mencken? Mencken? I never heard of him, but he's just some cheap jack trying to get a reputation by attacking me."

To Arnold Bennett, his proper place was in the music hall.

To Professor Pattee, a writer of the old school, he was a tempest in a beer mug.

To Ben Hecht, his one time contributor, now successful in films, he was a soap-box orator, street corner shouter and table thumper.

To a lady on a middle west paper, he was rude and insulting—"He might speak of our mental deficiencies with more restrained tone," she said.

A minister was grateful that he was not raised on Mencken but received his faith from the hickory stick.

To Gilbert K. Chesterton, he was a clever and bitter

Jew in whom a very real love of letters was everlastingly
exasperated by the American love of cheap pathos and
platitude. His philosophy was the sort of nihilistic pride
which belongs to a man with a sensitive race and a dead
religion.

A North Carolina lady said, "Away with the inhibi-
tion of inferiority this clever Hebrew would wish upon
us."

Accused of being one who disliked poetry, he defended
it. "I enjoy poetry when the mood of intellectual and
spiritual fatigue is on me. As an antidote against the insoluble riddle of existence, it is an escape from life. Even
Shakespeare I most enjoy, not on brisk mornings when I
feel fit for any deviltry, but on dreary evenings when my
old wounds are troubling me, and bills are piled up on
my desk and I am too sad to work."

With a strong clan feeling, he unites his family and
friends in a stand against the world. He is interested in
family trees, even if more dullness than talent hangs from
the wind-cracked branches.

An admirer of George Washington, he does not consider Theodore Roosevelt a great man.

Death causes him concern only in that it may prove
to be the final disintegration.

In high moments he is sure that all living is a goose-
step to the grave. Again, there are periods when he
pauses. Too shrewd to appeal to so rare a quality as

reason, the master of strong and beautiful prose will occupy an ironical niche in the long hall of posterity as one who preached against the democracy he loved to hate, and made vivid verbal war to shatter the illusions he enjoyed.